Schuylkill

Valley

Journal

Volume 49

Fall 2019

Patrons of *Schuylkill Valley Journal*

(contributions of $50 or more)

Subscriptions:

Single Issue: $10 or $13 (includes mailing)

1 year: $23 (includes mailing)

2 years: $45 (includes mailing)

Submissions: See page 147 for a complete list of guidelines.

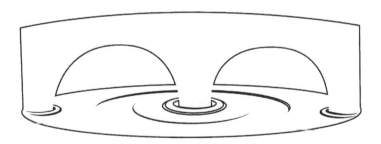

Cover images: Duck Girl
Sculptor: Paul Manship
Photographer: Ron Howard, Ed Hart

Founding Editor . . . . Jim Marinell

Publisher and Editor-in-Chief . . . . Peter Krok

Managing Editor. . . . . Mark Danowsky

Poetry Editor. . . . . .Bernadette McBride

Fiction Editor . . . . Fran Metzman

Flash Fiction Editor . . . . M.J. Iuppa

Arts Editor. . . . . David P. Kozinski

Contributing Writer. . . . . Mike Cohen

Contributing Writer. . . . . Ray Greenblatt

Contributing Writer. . . . . Eric Greinke

Editorial Assistant . . . . Jenna Geisinger

Online Architect/Producer . . . . Zoe Musselman

Tech Advisor . . . . Jordan Heil

Social Media Assistant. . . . . Cleveland Wall

Staff Photographer . . . . Ron Howard

Production Editor/Layout Design . . . . Ed Hart

Schuylkill Valley Journal is published twice a year,
and is also available online at
www.svjlit.com

Contents

Volume 49, Fall 2019

Poetry

Non-Fiction

Flash Fiction

WISE QUACKS

Mike Cohen

Our current sculpture adventure starts out like 'a walk in the park.' But as Connie and I enjoy a leisurely stroll through the hospitable confines of Rittenhouse Square, we come upon *Duck Girl*.

The girl is young and dressed in a diaphanous frock. She stands in the midst of a pool poised as if about to dip a toe into the water. She holds a duck in her arm. I would like to approach her, but in these days of vigilance against strange men in parks, I am hesitant. And though ducks are not as irascible as others such as geese, a pet can be overly protective of its owner. In this instance it would seem Connie would be far less likely to fall victim to fowl-play, so I ask her to go up to the girl and break the ice.

Duck Girl is situated on a limestone pedestal set in the Children's Pool of Rittenhouse Square. Connie gets as close as the pool will allow and gives the girl an irresistible smile. "I love your dress," Connie says politely. "It looks comfortable, and it's so pretty." Yet the girl's look remains tentative. The topic of fashion fails to draw the girl out. But while the duck girl is timid and reticent, the duck is anything but.

"What took you so long?" the duck squawks at Connie. "I understand you have been surveying sculptures around here for ten years. It's about time you got to the best of the lot."

Containing her surprise with composure, Connie engages the duck in conversation as if it were as natural to have a discussion with a bronze figure of a duck as it is to have one with a bronze figure of a person. "You are a fine piece of work," Connie admits. "But we've reported on some very significant statues: President Grant, General George Meade, Charles Dickens, Rocky Balboa…"

"I'll allow you Rocky," concedes the duck. "But as for the rest… As my maker, Paul Manship, said, *'It is sad to see our streets encumbered with hideous bronze gentlemen in badly modeled frock coats, on ugly pedestals.'* Paul tried to make up for that."

"He was a talented sculptor," Connie replies agreeably, "… the way he captured your girl's careful tread, her gentle face, her delicate dress…"

"Well pluck my pinfeathers!" exclaims the duck. "Leave it to *you people* to fawn over *you people*! It figures that the *human* figure gets all the human attention. You should hear how some folks fuss about my girl's scanty clothing and the 'wardrobe malfunction' leaving one breast exposed. But what about me? Here I am naked as a jaybird and nobody seems to notice—no humans, that is. The birds do. All the birds in Rittenhouse Square admire my good looks and know this sculpture as the Girl *Duck*, putting the emphasis where it belongs—on me!"

"But the sculptor was human," Connie reasons with the duck. "So the sculpture figures to be done from a human point of view."

"Paul Manship?" quacks the duck. "He was unusual. Some people might call him an odd duck, which is actually more complimentary than they imagine. Paul was very open-minded for a human. As you can see, he made *me* the center of this sculpture."

Making no comment, so not as to put the duck off, Connie cannot help but raise an eyebrow at this last remark.

Noticing this, the duck goes on to drive home his point, "The girl is just window-dressing, a bit of feminine fluff to pander to the aesthetic sensibilities of a mammalian public. But I'm the focal figure here. Don't take my word for it. Paul himself confided to me, *'I'm not especially interested in anatomy... what matters is the spirit which the artist puts into his creation—the vitality, the rhythm, the emotional effect.'* That's me he was talking about. I'm 'the vitality, the rhythm, the emotional effect' of this sculpture. It's as clear as the bill on my face! I only wish Paul could be here to tell you today."

Although Manship died in 1966, Connie realizes that ducks—particularly bronze ones—have long memories and deep attachments. "I am sorry for your loss," she says solemnly. "It's sweet that you seem to have genuine feelings for your sculptor. I'm sure he was dear to you. I suppose you know a lot about him."

"Sure do," crows the duck. "Paul was born in 1885, the youngest of a flock of seven siblings. His native state of Minnesota is home to a vibrant duck community, so he came by his interest in ducks naturally. He tried painting but upon finding he was colorblind, he turned to sculpture. He studied at the Art Students League of New York at age 20 and six years later reached the pinnacle of his career."

Connie asks, "Really? What was that?"

"Do I have to tell you?" remarks the duck. "The creation of *me* was clearly the defining moment of the sculptor's life, of course."

"Sorry," Connie apologizes, "we mammals aren't very intuitive."

"Clearly," chides the duck. Then he goes on, "Paul won the Widener Gold Medal in 1914 thanks to me."

"But he made other fine sculptures afterward," Connie points out, "… the *Prometheus Fountain* at Rockefeller Center, *Time and Fates Sundial* and *Moods of Time* sculptures for the 1939 New York World's Fair, *Aero Memorial* at Logan Square. He was prolific and influential. They say he got his ideas from what he saw of classical sculpture during his three year internship at the American Academy in Rome."

"I'll tell you what impressed him most in Rome," declares the duck. "He visited the Trevi Fountain. There, flapping about the water was a duck—a sight that was imprinted on his mind."

"He did fine work with duck and other animal figures," Connie admitted. "But he did so much more. Manship is a sculptor who helped art out of the Beaux Arts rut. He developed a simpler form for classical figures. He didn't go along with the abstract trend of the time but became a forerunner of the whole Art Deco movement."

"Art Deco, my tail feathers! Paul was an Art Duck-o sculptor first and foremost! By the webs between my toes, I was his high-water mark! The rest of his career was all momentum. Believe me," declares the duck, "mine are the wings above his wind."

Resources

Penny Balken Bach. *Public Art in Philadelphia*. Philadelphia,PA. Temple University Press, 1992

https://americanart.si.edu/artist/paul-manship-3096

https://en.wikipedia.org/wiki/Paul_Manship

an excerpt from Mark Lyons' novel

HOMING

a memoir

Nest Egg [Summer, 1957]

Sunset Beach. We're here for our yearly June vacation, in a blue clapboard house peeling from the salt, the waves a constant rhythm in our ears. Our family memories seem to be organized by a calendar of summer vacations, as if we use our time together at the beach to collect the memories of the previous year and fix them, a family photograph: the year of the summer vacation after Dad changed jobs, the summer vacation after Mom and Dad founded the Downey Community Players, the summer after Michele was born, the summer Bill was almost hit by a car that plunged into the lagoon where he was swimming, the summer of the all-time Grunion Run, the summer I found my first pubie, the summer of my parents' twentieth anniversary. This is the summer my mother returned from the mental hospital.

My mother has been home for two weeks now. She wanted to cancel our beach vacation, but Dad convinced her it would be good for her spirits. Our beach house has a white wicker chair in the corner of the living room, its back to the bay window that faces the ocean. Dad found a TV dinner table in a closet and parked it next to her chair, for her whodunits and coffee and cigarettes. Mom doesn't go outside to sun herself anymore and refuses to visit beach friends we've made over our last ten vacations. She won't even go to her favorite restaurant, Sam's Seafood, for swordfish to celebrate their anniversary. The big bash annual Little Theater Party and Grunion Run has been canceled; visitors are not welcome. My mother has become a hermit whose daylight life is filled with simple routines divided with by-the-clock doses of medicines. Reading an old Agatha Christie, asking Dad to warm her coffee, lighting a cigarette, playing solitaire, eating her sweet roll or sandwich from a paper plate, rocking back and forth until her eyes close and she slumps. Then she checks the clock, asks where her medicine is, Dad fetches it, and the Agatha/coffee/solitaire/food/rock/slump/sleep/medicine cycle starts over again. She goes to bed early now, sometimes before the sun sets; then Michele and I may toss sea shells into a hat or play indoor basketball before I read her a story. My brother occasionally comes down for the day; it's a short drive from his apartment in Long Beach. He's gained a little weight—he works all night in a doughnut shop.

Most nights I awake to the sounds I hate: the shuffling, desperate begging, denials, until my father's voice weakens and breaks. Now I hear something new: my father quietly sobbing as he gives in to my mother. Then the sound of medicine bottles being sorted, a glass being filled from the tap, gulping of pills on the back of her tongue. Two defeated shadows scuffle down the hall to the bedroom. Silence. Dad gets up at six a.m., starts coffee, lines up Mother's pills on the TV table, sneaks out to get an *L.A. Times* to read before his day starts, reads the front page and chugs one more gulp of coffee as Mom shouts *Bill! . . . Bill!* from her bed, *Bill!! . . . I need my pill!* A variation on the medicine ritual that now defines their lives, her new morning pill—some kind of upper to jump-start her from the drowsiness of last night's three a.m. trip to the medicine cabinet. She takes it before she can get out of bed.

Mornings I try to get Dad to play catch in the sand or challenge him to a cribbage match in the sun, but he finds reasons not to play, mostly says he can't leave Mother alone in the house. *Well, can't she come and sit in the sun? Well, she doesn't seem to want to do that, I know it would be good for her, I'll ask her.* He goes into the house and doesn't return, I know she has said no. Mom is afraid to come out of the shadows, and she and Dad have made a pact that he will stay in the shadows with her.

Tuesday, we've been here four days. I've been diving under the nine-foot high-tide waves, and after fifteen minutes am shivering uncontrollably, a reminder of how skinny I am. I dry myself off and come into the house to fix my favorite sandwich, mustard between slices of white bread. My parents are sitting in the living room, like maybe I walked in on a conversation. "HiDad, HiMom, anyone want some Coke? I'm getting myself one from the fridge." No answer. "*Hello?* Anybody home?" Silence. I try to make eye contact with my mother, but she won't look at me. I look over at my father. "What's up?"

"*Please . . .*," Dad says with an urgent tone, though he doesn't raise his voice.

"Please what?"

"Mark, I think it's best that you go outside or to your room."

"Outside? I just came inside. Why should I go back outside? And my room's dark." I'm trying not to sound angry; but, then, I don't care if I sound angry.

"Bill . . . *please . . .*" My mother's voice has a tinge of terror in it. She still won't look at me.

"Mark, I need you to leave the room. Now." My father's *Now* is quiet and firm; no doubt, it's an order. Pleading, too.

No way do I want to be sucked into this scene. "OK, just let me get a sandwich and a Coke. I'll eat it outside." In thirty seconds, I slap together my sandwich, toss the yellow-bladed knife into the sink, and uncap a Coke. I slam the screen door behind me to let them know I'm tired of this shit. I doubt they notice.

It's about 3:30 now. Late enough for shadows, but still hot enough to take off my shirt. My favorite time of day. I head north up the beach, the diffuse sun on my left still too high to be a ball, a slight breeze picking up off the water. I move down the slope of beach to the hard surface of cold sand left by the receding tide, check my back pocket to be sure I have my inhaler, and break into a slow trot, feeling the wet sand suck at my feet. I tuck my tee shirt into the back of my trunks. Past the brown-shingled house of Nellie and Chuck Fitz, friends of my parents, whose daughter Sandy tried to kiss me last summer (almost the summer of my first kiss, but by the time I figured out what she was up to she changed her mind). Past the light blue water tower landmark with *Sunset Beach* painted in four-foot-high red letters visible from the peak of Highway 101 in Belmont Shore. Past Eighth Street, which runs across the Pacific Coast Highway to the lagoon where I catch turtles, past the sign pointing to *Sam's Seafood Family Dining at Its Best.* I stop: I have never been this far up the beach. New territory.

I keep walking, another mile or so. The sun slips behind some finger clouds, the air turns cool, I put on my tee shirt. Beyond the last beach house are monstrous gray smokestacks that jut out of the sand, the tallest coughing up white smoke that turns pink, rises, disappears. I am a little spooked, like I'm about to cross an invisible border to another country. Where am I? I almost turn back, a return to familiar landmarks, then sight a ten-foot-high chain-link fence, topped by rusted barbed wire, that runs from the Pacific Coast Highway a half mile up to my right, across the beach in front of me, and disappears into the water a hundred yards offshore. I approach the fence cautiously. Maybe it's a prison wall, danger on the other side. I look for guards, careful not to touch the wire, it may be electrified. Then a peeling white plywood sign with black stenciled lettering announces:

No Trespassing
Government Property
US Naval Air Station
No Trespassing

I eye the colossal smokestacks through the fence: U.S. Navy destroyers, cruisers, one mammoth sleeping aircraft carrier. I recognize them from my father's World War II magazines I found in a barrel in the garage with cartoons about Japs with drooling teeth. The naval shipyard. Two hundred yards from the fence, the shore between the giant ships and me is lined with eight-foot-diameter gray steel spheres, stacked like cannon balls in old Civil War photos—the buoys which were used to string anti-submarine nets up and down the coast during the War. The *rrrrrrrr-chunk—rrrrrr-chunk—rrrrr-chunk* of a giant crane loading wooden netted crates onto a navy cruiser—probably headed for U.S. occupation forces in Korea. Waves lap at the chain-link fence, the sun takes shape as it begins its descent into the sea, still thirty-five degrees from the horizon. There are no people, no one to see me. I tap the fence with gritted teeth, leaning away: it's not electrified. I pry a three-foot-long two-by-six driftwood board with sea-etched grain out of the sand, and dig along the bottom edge of the metal fence, above the tide line where the sand is soft and dry. The board isn't very efficient, so I get down on my knees and paddle the sand between my legs with my hands, a dog looking for its buried bone. It takes five minutes to excavate a passageway under the fence to the other side. Lie on my back, drop my head into the hole, ease my arms under the fence and grab it from the other side, lower myself down now, slowly curving my body so my back matches the contour of the bottom of the hole and my chest doesn't scrape on the metal prongs of the fence. I catch my kneecap on the fence as I push myself clear, a two-inch scratch that will leave a scab.

I slide behind an old driftwood piling deposited on the upper sand by the high tide. The piling is snapped off at the base, half covered with black hairy mussels, some open revealing orange-pink flesh, a trace of fish-rot in the air. I gaze out over the metal and sand and water to make sure that no one has seen me. A tugboat moves up the channel on the other side of the buoys, its deep bellowing horn signaling something to the dock. The gray navy ships have taken on a pink tone, reflecting the sun. For a long time, I just crouch there in the cover of the piling, surveying this new territory parcel by parcel, alert to details, objects, colors, sounds. Piles of driftwood jammed against the jetty that forms the channel, bent pipes and wire jutting out of the sand like a no-man's land. Yellow and green and clear shards of glass from shattered bottles surround the base of a metal oil drum on which sits a beer bottle with its neck missing; probably used by someone for target practice. Thirty-foot leafy strands of salt-stinking seaweed cooking in the sun, stranded by the high tide. No footprints. It looks like nobody's been here for twenty years.

Then the scolding screech I recognize from my ten summers at the beach: a herring gull shadow appears on the sand, followed by the snapping of wings as the bird comes into view and settles on a hummock thirty yards in front of me. The seagull seems aware of the presence of a yet invisible intruder, and nervously turns its head around 180 degrees, scanning the area with orange eyes. The bird then walks directly to a place in the sand, a crevice, eases itself down, and carefully arranges something beneath its breast with its yellow beak. Everything in order, the gull again surveys the surroundings and, finding nothing changed, sits motionless, still uneasy, listening.

I have unearthed a seagull nesting ground.

A bird's nest is my favorite find. During breeding season, I secretly follow our yard birds in flight, beaks full of twigs or worms or insects, and discover where they nest: the finely woven oriole baskets hanging from the sycamore tree, the starlings and blackbirds screeching in the fronds of the eighty-foot palm tree in the corner of our yard, the screech owl in the hollow of the crab apple tree along the back fence line, the mud nests of robins and straw nests of mourning doves in the old thick spruce in the front yard. English sparrows in the flaming oleander bush, mockingbirds in the apricot trees, mud houses of barn swallows under the eaves of the garage. I know where the birds nest at our old elementary school—recess discoveries—and I've found the secret nests of the birds who inhabit the belfry of the Presbyterian Church where I play football on the front lawn and occasionally visit services, especially if Ann Hegardt is feeling religious that week. Crows nest in the evergreens that are windbreaks for the orange grove I walk through on the way to school, where the orchard smudge pots are foundations for kestrel nests, the irrigation dikes homes for kingfishers. Phoebes nest high in the mimosas, near the trunk, on the golf course where Dad and I play pitch and putt. And now I discover that seagulls nest at the far end of Sunset Beach, way past the water tower, beyond the chain-link fence, an hour from any swimming beach that I know.

I slowly rise from my hiding place behind the broken piling, and the seagull instantly lifts straight up into the wind, squawks loudly to draw my attention, glides point-winged wide-tailed past me, alights on a rock twenty yards down shore. The gull screeches frantically as I walk deliberately toward its shallow nest. Now it takes off from the rock and circles fifteen feet over my head, threatening, flapping its wings loudly, feigning dive-bombs, trying to drive me away. I carefully sink to my knees to inspect the clutch of four eggs. The bird can no longer endure the threat to its clutch and swoops down, beak aimed at my head. I tumble over on my side to avoid the attack, sand on my cheek as the bird arches up into the wind, readying for another assault. In a crouch I scuttle to my piling, sideways like a crab, and watch the bird circle the nest twice and nervously settle.

A sad feeling, that this is my one encounter with this hidden place where most likely I will never return. I need a souvenir from this beach, something to take with me so I don't forget, something that will make it easier for my memory to return.

An egg.

In all of my discoveries of active nests I have never touched them or their contents, afraid that the birds will desert their eggs. My plan is to find an abandoned nest—no interference with nature there. I come to a small rise with occasional tufts of sharp spiked grass, a young dune, behind which I hear chaotic squawking and flapping of a hundred gulls air-bound: a nesting colony. Before the gulls have a chance to group themselves and organize an attack, I slither down the slope of the dune and quickly find what I am look- ing for: a deteriorated nest, with no bird scat and one discolored egg barely visible beneath unkempt twigs. The egg is stone-cold, definitely not being incubated. I grab the egg with a handful of sand and snapping sticks, turn and charge over the dune, pursued by winged shadows. The birds become silent as the intruder disappears.

Panting in the shadows of the piling, I inspect my prize. I shake it, hold it up to the sun, tap it, look for cracks, smell it, heft it in my palm, feel its surface with my cheek. A keeper.

The sun is an orange ball, an inch above the horizon, as I locate the passageway under the chain-link fence. First, I reach under the fence with my left hand, carefully placing the egg on the other side on top of my tee shirt. I lower myself down into the hole, pull myself up on the other side, and shake the sand out of my shirt before putting it on. Make a plow of my hands and fill the passageway with sand, casually place some driftwood and twigs over the hole for camouflage, and return to my egg. As I start back up the beach, I turn to look through the fence beyond the parched and peeling *No Trespassing* sign. Looking for things to remember, like taking photos when you say good-bye.

I am glad to have a long walk home, more than an hour back down the lapping low-tide beach, the sun-ball now sunken below the horizon, orange and pink flames in the sky. The breeze has settled down, waves quiet and flattened. My ten summers at the beach have been filled with great discoveries: the red tide with the phosphorescent sand exploding when stomped, beached hammerhead sharks sucking air, thrashing when touched with a stick, a barracuda arching on the end of Dad's fishing line cast from the shore, manta rays gliding on the blue-green sea surface, abalone shells with their chips of mother-of-pearl. Digging for soft-shelled sand crabs, learning to swim in the safety of the lagoon across Highway 101, to dive under the crashing waves or to ride them two hundred feet to shore. The turtles and heron rookery I discovered with Chick Fitz, brother of Sandy who almost kissed me, when we waded neck-deep into the marshy backwaters beyond the lagoon. Flying fish and the spumes of the whales migrating south for the winter seen from the bow of the boat bound for Catalina Island. The world of crabs and insects and shellfish carried in the roots of giant kelp ripped from the bottom of the ocean in a recent storm, the fleeting captive tide-pool world of urchins and anemones and minnows. Learning to tell time by the tides. The magic of the grunion hunt and the great feast that followed. But the egg is my own find, a jewel snuck across the border. I'm making plans for the egg.

About The Novel:

In *Homing*, a heart-twisting memoir by Mark Lyons, published by New Door Books, a teen boy is the object of his mother's deep sexual urges. Does it cross the line into abuse? Is he responsible for her frequent retreats to mental hospitals? Can he ever forgive her? The son needs most of a lifetime to unravel, then free himself from, the mysteries of her demise.

ROYALS

Josephine Tolin

The Prom Queen tilted the passenger seat mirror to examine her fake eyelashes. She'd glued them on that morning: a mistake. She should've applied foundation first. "Shit," she muttered as she picked at a finicky end, curled up and away from her lash line ever so slightly. "Shit, shit, shit."

It was then, before they crowned her Prom Queen, that she spilled ketchup on her dress in the Steak-n-Shake parking lot. Before they crowned him Prom King, the Prom Queen's ex-boyfriend ran inside for napkins and came back clutching a wad of toilet paper. The Prom Queen let her chest deflate as she remembered why they'd broken up in the first place. He couldn't do anything right.

On the other hand, he didn't look so bad in a suit. He'd swapped his glasses for contacts and shaved his pubic chin beard, for once. The Prom Queen hadn't wanted to go with him at all. She'd asked her friend Marcus to ask her so she'd have a reason to avoid her ex, but he'd caught wind of it before Marcus had the chance to decorate her locker with streamers and Reese's Peanut Butter Cups. Marcus was going to use them—the Reese's—to spell out 'PROM?,' he'd said. The Prom Queen hadn't bothered to remind Marcus she was allergic to peanut butter.

But the morning Marcus was supposed to ask for the Prom Queen's French-tipped-prom-date-pinky-promise, a note from the main office was delivered to her second period Spanish class. Her theater teacher wanted to see her in the auditorium, stat. She slung her tote bag over her shoulder and shrugged at a ponytailed friend when they made eye contact across the classroom. When the Prom Queen turned her back to snatch the hall pass from its hook, the friend went back to picking her cuticles. The teacher droned on about the pluperfect—in Spanish, the ploos-kwam-per-feck-toe. The Prom Queen thought it was stupid to learn words in a new language when she didn't even know them in English.

When the Prom Queen shouldered open the double doors to the auditorium, "Tiny Dancer" was playing over the intercom. The song reminded her of her dad, who drove his SUV around town with the windows cracked, even in the winter. Once, she'd told the Prom King her Family Road Trip Story, starring her brother, Marlin. Marlin hated Elton John and was prone to carsickness. Before she understood the carsick part, the Prom Queen had watched Marlin's vomit fly out the window as the family sped northbound on I-94 to their grandparents' house in Detroit, "Tiny Dancer" playing in the background. Wind immediately smacked the barf southbound, all over Marlin's face. All the Prom Queen could think at the time was, Elton John's not that bad. Her father flicked cigarette ash out the window as her mother turned around in the passenger seat. She blotted Marlin's face with tissues, the thin ones that come wrapped in rectangular plastic packages. "There, there," the Prom Queen's mother had crooned. "There there, there there."

The Prom King had laughed. "*That's* why it's your favorite song?" he'd asked. They'd been perched on barstools on the same side of his kitchen counter. He was leaning towards her, one hand on his chin, the other hand curled around his wine glass. His breath smelled like vodka and onions. His breath always kind of smelled like vodka and onions.

"Not exactly," said the Prom Queen. "No, not exactly." She didn't know how to explain why she liked this particular song more than all the others. It felt like trying to explain why she preferred the color purple to red, pizza to spaghetti. She just *did*. She sipped from her glass to see if she still hated the taste of white wine. She did. The Prom King studied her with his little blue almond eyes. The Prom Queen always thought his eyes were too close together. It was the only thing about him she found unattractive, besides the blond stubble that poked like needles when she kissed him.

"Mr. Katz?" called the Prom Queen. She tugged her jeans up by the belt loops. Prom diets may be difficult, but they make all the difference, she told herself. "Mr. Katz? You wanted to see me?" The auditorium walls were painted red. The floor was the same shade, webbed with gray flowers that reminded the Prom Queen of cheap motel carpet.

The lights over center stage dimmed. "Mr. Katz?" the Prom Queen tried again, before she slumped sideways in a scratchy chair, leaning into the wooden arm and stretching her legs across the seats next to her. The position wasn't as comfortable as it looked, but she thought if Mr. Katz came across her this way, she'd seem cool and relaxed, not at all freaking out about the possibility he knew she'd been high at theater practice yesterday. She exhaled out her nostrils and nibbled on her French tips, careful not to bite hard enough to break them.

Oh, how it feels so real...lying here...with no one near...

The Prom Queen hummed along absentmindedly. Before the chorus broke again, there was Mr. Katz, pushing a big wooden 'P' to stage right, veins snaking about his arms like vines. Someone in the sound booth cranked the volume.

Count the headlights on the highways...

There was Cassie, her theater friend, pixie cut bobbing into the Prom Queen's line of vision as she pushed the 'R' next to Mr. Katz, who was beaming at the Prom Queen with his arms crossed. The Prom Queen's body tensed. She sat upright as if by instinct. As if she could sense him, the Prom King, somewhere near her. They hadn't spoken in weeks at that point. Didn't Mr. Katz and Cassie—couldn't they see?

Rick and Emma brought out the 'O' and 'M,' respectively. The Prom King took his time with the question mark. He was a handy guy, but the Prom Queen still wondered how he'd done that—how he'd gotten the question mark's squiggle to balance atop the dot with space between. The song ended with scratching, and she heard feet padding down the sound booth stairs. Somewhere behind her, the auditorium door slammed. The Prom King motioned towards the big wooden question; towards the theater teacher, the theater friends. "Well?" he said. He cracked his knuckles, then held his hand out to the Prom Queen, his front-row audience of one. Mr. Katz, Rick, and Emma whispered as they single-file shuffled backstage. Cassie waited and watched for a moment before following them. The Prom Queen rose from her seat. From up on the stage, the Prom King made his case.

"I thought it just made sense, you know? You and me. Prom. One more time." His voice cracked a bit as he said the last part. The Prom Queen understood. She and Marcus would look funny together, and people would ask questions. People might think they were more than friends. Like moths to light, her body moved to the Prom King's.

The Prom Queen dabbed at her ketchupped dress with the toilet paper. The Prom King had wet it in the bathroom before bringing it out to her; yes, at least he'd done that. He looked at her with his close-set eyes and pulled a metal flask from his pants pocket. He took a swig and slid it back in. Bits of wet toilet paper flaked onto her dress as the Prom Queen dabbed and blotted. She thought about how girls can't store flasks in their pants; the pockets are too small.

"I brought these." The Prom King pulled two butcher-papered cubes from his cavernous pockets. He set one on his lap and handed the other to the Prom Queen, who'd tossed the wet toilet paper out the window seconds earlier. A man walked out of Steak-n-Shake, glanced down at the wad by the front wheel of his car, kicked it, and climbed into his Ford Taurus. A child with unblinking eyes stared at the Prom Queen from the back seat.

The Prom Queen waved. The child continued to stare. She turned away to peel the paper from the cube. The Prom King had wrapped it like a present, fastening Scotch tape along the paper's creases and folds. The Prom Queen smiled at this as her fingers went. Maybe he really was trying.

The Prom King had tried a lot harder at first. When they'd started dating at the beginning of junior year, he'd taken the Prom Queen on a date to the 49er Drive-In, packing the trunk of his Oldsmobile with blankets and pillows, popcorn and Snickers bars. "Peanuts," she'd reminded him when she saw the Snickers.

"Right," he'd said, palming his forehead. He chucked the Snickers over the backseat headrests, reaching an arm across the Prom Queen's shoulders. His leather jacket was coated in Axe body spray, she'd noticed. It wasn't a good smell or a bad smell. She'd leaned into him then, pulling a down comforter over her bare legs. Hundreds of bodies freckled the lawn; entire families crammed together in car trunks, young lovers swaddled in blankets with their temples pressed together. The Prom King passed the popcorn as lights faded above the giant screen. The Prom Queen crammed her hand in the bucket, shoving a heap of buttery kernels into her mouth. A couple of yellow pieces flew out as she chomped. The Prom King laughed, holding her closer. Molly Ringwald stepped onto the screen, small and petite with her collarbones peeking out above a pink V-neck. The Prom Queen nuzzled her face into the Prom King's bicep. She felt small next to him—delicate, like Molly.

She'd considered herself lucky then, in that old car with that large man. This was the stuff of the '80s movies her parents had shown her. She'd always been nostalgic for an era she'd never known, when men in leather coats held boomboxes outside windows. She leaned in to kiss the Prom King, bumping the popcorn bucket and spilling all over the trunk.

The Prom Queen balled the butcher paper in her fist, abandoning it in a cup holder. On her knee, she balanced a brownie. She'd been high before—yes, of course she had. She'd been high so many times, but never from ingesting something. "Well?" said the Prom King. "We gonna eat these, or what?"

"Who'd you get them from?" she asked, pinching off a corner.

"Cassie," said the Prom King. "Who else?"

It was true—the Prom King always bought his drugs from Cassie. She was a friend of the Prom Queen too, of course. But Cassie's loyalty had always been with the Prom King, the Prom Queen thought as she shoved a brownie chunk into her mouth. She grimaced. It tasted the way skunk smells. More pot than brownie. The Prom King was licking his lips. He'd devoured his brownie in a couple bites. "So good," he said, cracking his knuckles. "So, so good." He leaned into the Prom Queen's shoulder with his mouth still half-full, kissing her lightly on the neck. She clenched her jaw, then unclenched it when she realized she was clenching it.

"We should get going," said the Prom Queen. The Prom King nodded, popping in a cassette tape she'd made him for his birthday. The Oldsmobile sputtered to life. He pushed his gelled hair out of his face and maneuvered the sofa-car out of the parking lot.

They were lucky, the Prom King and Queen. It was the first year the school had decided to move prom to an off-campus location; before that, it'd been in the school cafeteria. This year, the dance would be held at the Orak Shrine in Michigan City. The Shrine's logo was a picture of a bearded man wearing a fez. Someone—probably Cassie, Student Body President—had copied the fez man onto the ticket template. The Prom Queen pictured Cassie standing by the printer in the main office as it pumped out tickets she'd designed, chatting up the principal, telling him all about her lead role in the upcoming play. Cassie would be Sandy in *Grease*. The Prom King would be Danny. The Prom Queen had been assigned the role of Nurse Wilkins. She held her prom ticket in her palm, tracing the fez with a white-tipped fingernail. Her face felt itchy, but she resisted scratching it. It was like holding her pee on a long family road trip, only worse. Under layers of blush and concealer, she felt a hotness spreading across her cheeks. Her nails were so long, so fake, so perfect for itch-scratching. She rested her chin on a fist and closed her eyes, trying to breathe deeply even though the air kept snagging in her throat.

"You okay?" the Prom King asked as he pulled into a parking space in front of the Orak Shrine. The Prom Queen nodded, closing her eyes. He stroked the Prom Queen's tingly face with the back of his hand, and she squeezed her eyes shut even tighter. The Shrine was a domed, stucco building with the paint peeling off. A man in a fez held the door open for the parade of prom pairs. Young women with spider-leg eyelashes had stuffed themselves into dresses two sizes too small, their breasts spilling over low-cut corset tops. The men all looked the same; black suits, black shoes, black ties. Some black-framed glasses here and there.

Cassie and Marcus strode arm in arm past the Oldsmobile's windshield, glancing backwards before whipping their heads right back around. Cassie's dress was green and puffy, her short hair congealed in a cloudlike mass. She was beautiful the way women in '50s movies are beautiful, and the Prom King watched them a little longer than was acceptable. The Prom Queen couldn't blame him, though. Her own sense of time was moving slowly, her motor functions lagging. She hadn't thought the edibles would kick in so quickly, but then again, what did she know? She unbuckled her seatbelt after fumbling for a minute with her too-long nails. *Don't touch your face,* she reminded herself as a colony of hives began to simmer under her skin, dormant for now. She glanced in the car mirror again. The finicky eyelash bothered her more now. It was all she saw when she looked at herself—just a fake eyelash, applied all wrong. As she stared at her reflection, she felt someone enter her periphery. She jumped. "Hi," said the Prom King, opening the passenger door and scratching his stubble-less chin. "We should go inside now."

The doorman glanced down at their tickets. Maybe he recognized himself in those two-dimensional fez men, floating among clunky letters that read, SHRINE ON! AT PROM. He glanced at the Prom Queen's swelling face, the Prom King's foggy eyes, then back down at the tickets. He motioned to the entrance. "This way," he told them. The ex-couple nodded. The Prom King reached for the Prom Queen's hand. She laced her fingers with his, her nails digging into his knuckles. She scratched at her throat with her other hand, leaving white nail trails on the red. Anything to keep her hands away from her face.

The dance floor was a banquet hall with the tables all pushed up against the walls. Fluorescent lights spun with hoop dresses. They spun with the Prom Queen, whose airway was closing fast. She dropped to her knees. "I can't breathe," she choked.

The Prom King squatted beside her. "You're just high, you know that? Okay, listen to me. Listen. You always do this. Just pull it together and listen to me." The Prom Queen's world was runny. Dresses bled like watercolors as they circled her, concerned friends crouching to see what was wrong, could she breathe, could she hear them? She could certainly hear Cassie, Student Body President. Cassie's voice, amplified by a microphone, even though it didn't need to be. Cassie's voice, announcing the new Prom King and Queen. Announcing—what?

The Prom Queen woke up in the hospital with an IV in her arm and a plastic tiara hanging from her hair by a comb tooth. Cassie and the Prom King were at her bedside. Their shoulders fell when she rolled to face them.

The Prom King's too-big dome crown had slipped over his forehead, nearly covering his eyes. Take it off, thought the Prom Queen.

Cassie squeezed the Prom Queen's hand. "We were worried about you."

"Yeah," said the Prom King. "You scared the shit out of us."

"We called your parents," said Cassie.

"Well, I did," said the Prom King. "They should be here any minute now."

"Any minute now," echoed Cassie. "I need to use the restroom." She patted the Prom Queen's hair as she stood. "You looked beautiful tonight."

"Thanks," said the Prom Queen. Cassie smiled and cocked her head, waiting for the 'you too' that would never come. Then she slipped out of the room, crunchy hair unmoving as she walked.

"I'm so sorry," said the Prom King, scooting his chair closer to the edge of the bed. "I had no idea there'd be traces of peanuts in the edibles. Neither did Cassie." He put his face in his hands, rocking back and forth, back and forth.

"What?" The Prom Queen rubbed her eyes. Fake eyelashes hung from the corner of her left eye. She pulled them off, hurling them on the tile near the Prom King's shoes. "Did the doctor say that's what it was? I thought maybe I was just—you know, I've never *eaten* weed before—"

The Prom King nodded slowly. Cassie re-entered the room and resumed her perfect posture in the chair next to the Prom King. The Prom Queen glanced down at their legs, which were touching at the knees.

"I'm interested in someone else," he'd confessed the night they made it unofficial, a couple of months before prom. "I can't see myself with you anymore, but the thought of you with anyone else—" The Prom King made a fist and shook it. The Prom Queen was silent. She leaned back, cranking open the window of the Oldsmobile. Her Speedway slushie sweated in its cup holder. She picked it up just to have something to do with her hands.

"One of my friends?" she asked at last. She hated the way her voice sounded then, all weak and raspy. A gull perched on the car's long hood, peering at the both of them through stupid eyes.

"No," said the Prom King, and the Prom Queen started to cry. "No, of course not!" Her sobs were coursing through her like blood now, shaking her. He grabbed her and pulled her in, squeezing as her tears soaked his t-shirt.

She let him hug her, let the tears run their course. She was angry. So angry. But the refrain in her head sang, *Hold me closer.* The Prom Queen didn't hug back.

Author's Note

"Royals" is mostly about prom. Prom itself is pretty interesting to me—it feels like a chance for high schoolers to make/unmake themselves, packaging the whole of their young romantic lives into posed photos and outrageous dresses. The Prom Queen—who, more than anything, wants an '80's romance like her parents'—realizes, as the story progresses, how impossible it would be for her relationship to live up to the ones she glorifies.

MINT GARDEN

Constance Garcia-Barrio

"I know I'm fifty cent short of the fare, driver, but I got no more money."
I turned my pocket inside out so she could see wasn't nothin' there but lint.
Course, I had two dollars in the other pocket, but I needed it to get back to
the shelter.

The driver cut her eyes at me, didn't say nothing, but she pulled off
from the curb like her tits afire, almost made me fall down in the aisle. I
found a window seat, put my nose to the glass to see the snug row houses in
the last of the light.

A while since I come to this part of town. Ray and me used to live near
here in a plain two-story brick house with a little fireplace. Nice neighbors,
but churchy. Lay a prayer on you in a minute. We had a front yard the size
of a pool table, but big enough to grow herbs—mint, basil, and rosemary—
upliftin' herbs. But my life gone slantwise since then. Hard to find a dry place
to sleep 'less I go to the shelter and say howdy to the mice.

Ray was a tall saddle-colored man who looked tasty as sin fried in
bacon fat. Didn't treat me rough 'cept now and then. He had winnin' ways.
One time, he made me cologne with rosewater and some secret oil. Sprayed
it on me in the mornin' so I'd carry his love with me all day. And nights, child,
my goodness! He would start nibblin' at my toes and work his way on up.

Before I married Ray my sister said, "He ain't worth a cracked piss pot,"
but listenin' to her is like emptyin' a dumpster direct into your head. She's
liable to say anything. With her garbage mouth and hangdown behind, she
can't hold on to a man. I told her, "You just jealous."

By and by, after Ray and me got married, he gambled away our savings.
Tried to hide it at first, but we lost our car, then the house. Never will forget
the rainy mornin' the sheriff and his men put us out. Neighbors was lookin'
on. Old Miss Kershaw five doors down smiled all over herself. Never could
stand her, looks like Frankenstein dyin' of small pox.

What I'm sayin', I ain't a fool, I saw where things was headed well before
I sat on the curb 'longside my cook pots. If only I hadn't loved Ray so.

Driver, driver! Let me off the next stop.

I don't come 'round here 'cept at sundown. Enough light then to see my
old house without jelly-butt Kershaw spyin' me. I came by one time at noon,
and she caught me grubbin' in my old garden 'cause nothin' feels better than

earth in my hands. At first, she didn't recognize me with these raggedy-ass clothes and five missin' teeth. When she realized it was me she called the cops. Another time, she sicced her dog on me. But I can still throw a hard stone. Hit that dog in the snout so hard you could hear him yelp halfway to Georgia. 'Magine tryin' to run me out my yard!

Now, if I can just eat me a few leaves of mint before it dies back, I'll make it through the winter. The taste goes into me like a green blessin' I can keep callin' up till spring.

Here's the place. Wait a minute. This the right house? New paint, but it's the right number. Where's my garden at? Shit! Is this cement? Lord Jesus, nothin' but a cement patio here now.

Author's Note

I have a friend who sleeps on porches and in shelters, but has remained sassy in spite of hard living. The story also honors the special place of mint in African American history. "In 1792, a man, aged 72, was cured of the stone by taking the expelled juice of red onions and horse mint…" says Samuel Stearn in *American Herbal or Materia Medica*, 1801. "The discovery was made by a Negro in Virginia, who obtained his freedom thereby." In addition, in the Yoruba religion, a sister tradition to Vodun, or Voodoo, mint is said to attract good fortune.

JOHN "TUBBY" STOVER

Arthur Davis

The man most called "Tubby" Stover sat on the street corner counting his toes. It was his third attempt, and he couldn't make sense of the number of filthy buds protruding from the top of his shoeless feet.

There couldn't be eleven, he reasoned, and tried again, ignoring the ebb and flow of those who passed by the fat man sitting on the curb wearing an unbuttoned, blue work shirt and plaid boxer underwear clearly visible through ragged work pants.

Tubby couldn't have known Ricardo Figueroa was watching him from the seclusion of his second-story office above Fifth & Royal.

Figueroa switched off his ornate, brass desk lamp, a gift from his banker, and made his way down the stairs and out onto the street. Having started out dealing drugs in the neighborhood schoolyards, with a gift for melodrama and deceit, over the years he had become one of the most successful businessmen in Westvale, California.

He supplied the local utility with unskilled, non-union, immigrant day-workers who, in turn for the drudgery, were eager to kick back part of their salary to him through one of his other enterprises.

Dozens of cars a day taken from the streets in southern California found their way to his chop shops outside Westvale. He controlled two of the largest messenger services in the county, through which drugs and the most potent opioids were distributed.

"Hey, Tubby," Figueroa asked, making sure not to frighten the man who was rocking absently back and forth on the curb, and whose sensibilities were known to be as unpredictable as his fits of anger. "It's me."

The big man pulled away sharply without looking up.

"It's Ricardo. We went to school together, man."

Tubby shifted about and brought his feet up under his buttocks as the strange man hovered above him. Now he would never know how many toes he had. "Go away."

"Tubby, it's Ricardo? Ricardo Figueroa? We went to school together. We played baseball and were in a history class together? You wrote a great paper on the Civil War? Come on man, you know me."

"Go away," he repeated loudly, suddenly remembering the exact day he overcame the demons that once cursed him with a thirst for alcohol and crack cocaine. The struggle had taken half a decade and left him fragile, fearful, and hostile.

"Would you like a meal and a clean place to sleep tonight?" Figueroa asked, dropping a ten-dollar bill and small white card in his lap.

Bryant Avenue Men's Shelter the card read. Under the printed address, the man had written his name and a time. *Nice handwriting*, Tubby noticed.

He once took pride in his handwriting, remembering a small, crowded classroom. He was hunched over a test. He had studied every night for days in preparation. When the exam was over he received the second highest grade. It would be the first of many experiences that, regrettably, he was unable to parlay into a normal life.

Tubby drifted by storefronts, pausing like a curious child would right before Christmas so that the half-mile trip took nearly two-hours. Terrible things happened to people in shelters. He had heard stories of abuse and perversion, of being held for days and weeks against your will, and worse.

* * *

"No, officer, I had no idea what he was going to do. How could I? I spotted him sitting on the curb, remembered how great a guy he was in school, and in a moment of weakness that looking back now was a stupid mistake, I gave him ten dollars and a card from a shelter I had helped support and told him to get himself together. He gave me a hard time," Ricardo Figueroa said over and over until he had refined his speech to the police so that he would be comfortable with it when he was questioned. "Of course I had no idea. I was only trying to help the guy out."

A perfect blend of sympathy and regret, Figueroa concluded from his office window and made two phone calls that he hoped would seal the fate of one of his most pernicious enemies.

* * *

Tubby stood across the street and watched two men enter the shelter, half expecting them to be chased back out by a band of pitchfork-wielding demons.

He made it across the street and signed in, was given a towel, a cake of soap, and told to leave his clothes in a metal basket.

The facility was brightly lit and the bathing area was clean and open, with only low stall partitions ensuring both safety and privacy. Three other men were taking their time under the steaming hot water that cascaded down on their worn, rank frames.

Tubby suddenly became conscious of his size. At one point in his life, he had been a fair outfielder. Having just managed to work himself free from the grip of drugs, he couldn't imagine what it would take to lift himself out of the gutter of a pointless existence.

He took his time in the shower, noticing that the scent of the soap was mildly sweet, then rinsed off and realized he had left the ten-dollar bill in his pants pocket.

"You're new here," one of the attendants said and handed him the basket filled with his warm, freshly washed, clothing. "We have a cool little machine here that washes and dries small loads in under ten minutes."

He slipped them on, jammed his hand into his warm pants pocket, and retrieved the damp, crumpled, ten-dollar bill and worn little white card.

"You know mister Figueroa?" an attendant asked, reviewing the list of recent walk-ins.

Tubby quickly shook his head. He didn't recognize the name and knew better than to admit to knowing. When you lived on the street, the only name you had to remember was your own, and volunteering even that could cause you a world of regret.

He was given a tray with a bowl of soup and tasty meat sandwich and cup of coffee.

Several men were watching a detective series on the TV. Besides food and shelter, Tubby missed his beloved crime and police dramas. If he took pride in anything, it was the satisfaction he got from predicting the ending of the most impenetrable mystery.

"Would you like to sleep here tonight?" the same attendant asked.

"A bed?"

"A clean bed."

Tubby nodded. "Yes. Please."

"Be back by nine tonight or we'll give it to someone else."

By the time he arrived in front of the two-story building that housed a law office on the first floor and a suite of small offices on the second, John Stover was more conscious of those he had offended, abandoned, of the opportunities he had squandered, of the life he had wasted and for caring so little about those who had sacrificed so much on his behalf.

The sign on the door at the end of the second floor corridor read *Ricardo J. Figueroa, Investment Advisor.*

"There you are," Ricardo said coming around to the front of his desk.

The office was furnished with two enormous leather couches and a mantle hanging over a fake fireplace on which stood a row of gold and silver sports trophies.

John felt a fearful shift deep within his gut.

The opposite wall was covered with dozens of awards for community work, placards, and photos of the man shaking hands with prosperous and obviously politically connected people.

"Well, how are you feeling?"

"Okay," John answered. This man seemed larger than the one who had loomed over him as he sat in the gutter.

"That shelter is an amazing place, isn't it?"

"It's new?"

"Almost a year and cost a fucking fortune, I can tell you. I had to convince half the people in this town to accept such a facility. Then I worked with those filthy, bloodsucking politicians to get the ordinances approved," he said moving to the wall of memorabilia. "And as you can see," he said, pointing to a photo of eight men standing in front of the shelter cutting a blue ribbon dedicating the facility, "I finally managed to get it built."

"It's nice," John finally said, silently hoping that a modest demonstration of appreciation would be all that would be required of him.

"Look at them," Ricardo said moving to the window behind his desk. "Hundreds and hundreds of people moving about, doing their daily chores, going to work, buying food, longing for a drink if they had the money. Every day a hard-won victory just to stay alive. It's not easy. I know you know that."

As the man continued, John caught a glimpse of Ricardo Figueroa's profile and was suddenly jolted back two decades to his tenth-grade history class and the kid who sat next to him who cheated on his tests and took pleasure in turning student against student.

It was Ricardo Figueroa. *My God*, John gasped in silence. If only the man knew to whom he had given a few hours' respite.

"Well, we got you bathed and a good meal. It's a start."

John nodded agreeably.

He was reliving an incident that happened at the beginning of his eighth grade. Ricky Figueroa had a brand-new, three-ring binder filled with sheets of fresh white paper, complete with brightly colored subject separators. John's was three years old and falling apart.

Before the day was over John learned that a similar binder was stolen from another eighth grader. When confronted by the assistant principal Ricardo insisted his father had just bought it.

From that day on every kid in the school respected Ricky Figueroa, not for his academic achievements but for his defiance in the face of the fact that his father had been killed by a drunk driver a year earlier.

"You ever heard of Congressman Billy John Johnson?"

"No. Never."

"Well, I seem to have gotten myself in a bind, trying to do good, actually, and I thought—and you should know that you don't have to do this—you might be able to help me out."

Congressman Billy John Johnson, the paragon of business prudence and ethics, was urging the United States District Court for Southern California to investigate Figueroa's government contracts. Johnson commanded great respect and his superior character was held hostage in a body so compromised by time and a litany of ailments that Ricardo Figueroa guessed all it would take to bring it to a state of absolute failure was a small, well-placed shock.

"Is that why you sent me to the shelter?"

"My, no! Certainly not. I thought you could use a hand."

John wondered what it would be like to wear such an expensive suit. "What do you want?"

"I'll give you a hundred dollars to get Billy John Johnson's briefcase."

A briefcase? John asked himself incredulously. *What could be in such a briefcase, and why him?* "I'm not a criminal."

"Johnson has something that belongs to me, and I have no way to get it back but to take it from him. It's an early edition of *Huckleberry Finn.* You may not consider a book so valuable, but I do. I loaned it to him months ago, more as a goodwill gesture, and he has refused every call I've made to return it. My attorney warned me that with all the community projects I'm sponsoring, like the shelter, I don't need publicity by taking the law into my own hands."

The visage of a bent old man wearing a white suit and white, wide-brimmed hat and chomping on a long black cigar while looking out over the wide expanse of the Mississippi from the bridge of a riverboat returned John Stover to a time when he took pride in the movement of his mind.

"Johnson is a collector of rare editions."

"Books?"

"A book," Ricardo answered, trying his patience. He was used to giving commands, not explaining himself. "A very special book."

Figueroa waved down to two women on the street dressed in flashy tightfitting leather skirts that left nothing to the imagination.

John knew who they were and how much each charged for a blowjob.

"Let me see here," Ricardo said flipping open a file that was sitting on his desk. "You were convicted of petty theft once, twice, no three times. The last time was last November. Overwhelming evidence on all counts, and I understand the police questioned you about your involvement in a burglary last year up in Lawrenceville."

The last time John Stover was so angered was after he had been beaten up by a gang of kids in junior high school. Three boys jumped him and stole his few dollars and his books, which were later found in the trash.

His mother cursed him for ruining his pants and the principal didn't even bother to question the three John had identified. It took him three years, eight inches and eighty pounds' growth before retribution was his.

One by one, he met them in the streets, in a parking lot, and with a small baseball bat, savaged each until all were hospitalized. That time John benefited from the failure of the system, as the police willingly looked the other way. Three of the most foul the neighborhood had produced had, through some miracle of reverse justice, been given a dose of their own viciousness.

"Now, John, please listen carefully," Ricardo began, knowing with Johnson's well-publicized congestive heart disease any sudden incident would probably kill the eighty-three-year-old "saint of the city," as the newspapers liked to call him.

John instinctively suspected the story about Johnson was a distraction from some greater evil Figueroa was plotting.

"Every Friday, Billy John Johnson leaves his home at exactly at 7:15 in the morning and walks the few blocks to his office at 333 Federal Plaza. I've been told he takes the book to work every day and reads a few chapters at lunch. You come up behind him, I think around Blakeley and Grove and grab his briefcase. He's a tough old bastard so be careful. Bounce him hard once or twice on the head so he knows you mean business."

"And?"

"And you get your hundred, and I get back my first edition."

"Why don't you ask one of your friends to do it?"

"I could. Absolutely. I could ask anybody, but I'm trying to help you," Figueroa insisted, finally questioning his own judgement in Stover.

"I see."

"You don't have to do a damn thing, John, though you shouldn't be so quick to turn down a favor from a man who could do you a world of good."

A flashy suit, a plush office, sweet cologne, slicked-back hair, and the glorified pimp thinks he can get you to strangle your own mother and be grateful for the opportunity?

The founders of this country knew the importance of laws. Samuel Langhorne Clemens wrote of the decency of man and spoke to it in both

Huck Finn and *Tom Sawyer*. "We are a nation of laws," John's history teacher would praise over and over, Stover recalled with a surge of pride, *"and that above all makes this country morally and spiritually unique."*

John Stover knew he broke the law because he was a weak man, not a morally corrupt man and never, except for those three boys, had he ever hurt one human spirit.

However, he was a realist. What difference did it make in this case? Another briefcase was another briefcase. John knew he would agree to the request, but the words hadn't quite formed on his lips yet.

"Now, frankly, if you can't do this simple thing for me, I might be persuaded that you're not a man to be trusted, not a man I would want back in my shelter."

"And you're going to give me a hundred dollars for the briefcase?"

Ricardo lifted a hundred-dollar bill from under the brass desk lamp and stuffed it into John's shirt pocket. "Whatever you do, don't damage the book, and don't let him spit on you."

John could feel the hundred-dollar bill scratch against his chest as if it were tearing the flesh from his soul. He desperately wanted a night of peace, but it was a poor man's trade-off for a future of fear and servitude to a man who he knew was pure evil.

Figueroa waited, with a combination of contempt and pity, knowing that with one phone call Stover could be deprived of every right he ever had. "Listen, Tubby, make up your mind. I haven't got all day. Take the fucking hundred, or take a hike."

John removed the hundred-dollar bill from his pocket and set it flat on Figueroa's desk, making sure to smooth out each wrinkled corner.

"What does that mean, you fat fuck? You think I'm kidding about what's going to happen if you walk away from this?"

John came up behind the desk next to where Figueroa was sitting, set one hand around Figueroa's throat while the other grasped the back of Figueroa's chair, slamming it up against the desk.

Figueroa tried to get loose, but John's position, weight, and strength gave him crushing leverage. Figueroa flailed a bit and managed a few garbled curses before he ran out of air and time.

John waited another full minute before releasing Figueroa, who slumped forward over against his desk.

Remembering how to deconstruct a crime scene, John grabbed Figueroa's fingers and scraped the polished fingernails across his own cheek, tore open his own shirt, and scattered the stacks of correspondence across the desk.

He clutched Figueroa's right hand around one of the many heavy paperweights and swung it against his right shoulder and, with his eyes closed, slammed it into his forehead until Figueroa's hand and his hand were covered in blood, then released it from the dead man's grip.

He removed Figueroa's wallet and scattered what had to be over a thousand dollars in all directions and checked the drawers for a gun.

John Stover grabbed Ricardo Figueroa and with almost effortless ease heaved the pale, limp body through the plate glass window that read, *Ricardo J. Figueroa, Investment Advisor.*

He moved back from the gaping, jagged glass opening knowing that Figueroa's jewelry, and whatever else was worth taking, would be picked clean before he rolled to rest.

Then he stumbled against the wall of photos so that his blood would mark a bright red smear as half the mementos shattered in different directions.

He then crawled to the window and called out for help.

"I was tired of his threats, and when he wanted me to kill a man, a Billy John Johnson, and said that he would have me raped and beaten if I returned to the shelter without doing as he wanted, he grabbed something and hit me and told me that I had no right to live at all and that I was a piece of shit and that I should be glad he was going to give me the chance to make some money. He got crazy! Wild! I knew he was going to kill me when I said no, so I grabbed him when he came at me and then, and then...," John said to a room full of spellbound detectives, "and he kept cursing me, and then that's all I remember."

His past, the assaults he endured in fact and in spirit, the looks of disdain and contempt, the feeling of self-loathing, the sense that his life was over before it began, the realization that as he sat on the street he was already dead and only living out his own funeral all vanished as the body of Ricardo Figueroa plummeted to the street below, a remorseless footnote to John "Tubby" Stover's barren, spiritless past.

Of course, this feeling of relief was told to no one, except many years later to a psychiatrist who was helping John deal with his relationship with his youngest son.

His wounds were bandaged and, after an examination at the hospital, he was taken to the police station and booked.

A public defender was appointed to his case. A clever little man with thick brown glasses and a sharp, convincing tongue who was well connected to Billy John Johnson. John Stover was soon granted bail after the charges were reduced to manslaughter because newly discovered evidence proved that Stover was only acting in self-defense.

"Every Friday, Billy John Johnson leaves his home at exactly at 7:15 in the morning and walks the twelve blocks to his office at 333 Federal Plaza. You come up behind him, I think around Blakeley and Grove. He's a nasty bastard so you need to make sure he's dead," John repeated frantically over and over, to anyone who would listen.

Knowing the intricacies of Johnson's daily routine made a difference to the District Attorney. A month to the day later, after a more thorough investigation, he was released after accepting a plea deal of involuntary manslaughter and given three years' probation.

Billy John Johnson made national news by offering the man who had saved his life a full-time job at the Bryant Street Shelter.

"If John Stover is ever threatened by anyone from anywhere, he has been instructed to call the police first and me second," Billy John Johnson detailed in the local press, expressing the sentiment of many in the community who had rallied around the homeless man who had put his life in jeopardy to save another.

The memory of Ricardo Figueroa was further tarnished by documents found by the police in his home that revealed the extent of his corrupt activities.

John Stover worked at the Bryant Street Shelter for nine years, attending college at night to earn his degree, which eventually allowed him to become manager of the facility and the master of his own life.

Author's Note

Years ago I was in Philadelphia and saw a man sitting on the street, his disheveled appearance, worn-though shoes and torn clothes, more a sign of the times you could see in any large city. It took me over a dozen years to craft a story around the impact that incident made on me, which is now *John "Tubby" Stover*.

PHILLY DRACULA

A Transylvanian count. A Pennsylvanian connection.

Matt Lake

When you think of Dracula, you may think of the Wallachian prince Vlad Tepeś from Transylvania. You may think of the suave Hungarian actor Bela Lugosi. You may think of Bram Stoker, the Irish theatrical manager who wrote the book. You may think of London or Whitby or Carfax Abbey, the English locations in the book. The one thing you probably don't think of in connection with Dracula is Philadelphia.

We're about to change that.

During the seven years that Bram Stoker worked on his most famous novel, he left a trail in the northeastern United States—not a bloody trail so much as a paper trail—and the trail had its epicenter in Philadelphia.

Although Bram Stoker was based in London, part of his duties included being a tour manager for Henry Irving's acting troupe, which made frequent visits during the 1890s to Broadway and beyond. Stoker made all the arrangements and traveled with them on their tours. During his off-hours, he was researching and revising and tweaking his vampire classic.

Philadelphia was a focal point of Stoker's American experience. He had been a huge fan of Walt Whitman during his college days, and he struck up a fanboy correspondence that lasted until the poet died in 1892. He found out that Whitman was then living across the river in Camden, NJ, and maneuvered hard to get an introduction to his hero. He got his wish through a prominent Philadelphia lawyer Thomas Corwin Donaldson, a friend of Whitman's who also handled his literary affairs.

Whitman and Stoker met at Donaldson's home in 1884, and the three were tight from that point on. Stoker trekked to Philly whenever he could.

THE LEGIONNAIRE'S DISEASE HOTEL

You can actually see part of the Dracula-Philadelphia connection today by setting up an appointment at the Rosenbach Library and Museum. This Philly institution purchased a large volume of Dracula notes from the Stoker estate shortly after Bram died, and the papers are available to researchers with an appointment. Dracula scholars have been doing this for years, and as they leaf through sheaves of mismatched paper, it doesn't take them long to notice the letterhead on one of the sheets. It's for the Strafford Hotel on Broad Street—the swanky hotel that later merged with the Bellevue to become the Bellevue-Strafford.

If that name sounds vaguely familiar, it's because in the 1970s, it played host to a convention of the American Legion, many of whose members contracted a mysterious new disease there. It wasn't vampirism: This ailment was given a name that acknowledged the fraternal order that first contracted it: Legionnaire's Disease.

A BARNSTORMING DRACULA DRAFT

Back in the 1890s, Bram Stoker's dealings with Thomas Corwyn Donaldson expanded into a literary relationship. Donaldson gave Stoker manuscripts from his hero Whitman. Stoker began opening up about the novel he was working on. Donaldson did groundwork for a publishing deal with Double-day to get Dracula published in the United States.

But like the ill-fated Lucy in the novel, Donaldson's days were numbered. He was ailing during Stoker's most productive period in finishing the novel, and didn't live to see the book's impact—he died during the slow year that followed the novel's publication.

But this is not the end of his connection with the Dracula story.

Fast-forward to the 1980s, and Donaldson's heirs are hanging out on the family farm in northwestern Pennsylvania. Two of them decide to clear out the junk in one of the barns, and haul out three trunks. The first one they opened contained some personal belongings that look like they were dumped out of a desk drawer. Then they drag out a large bundle of type-written papers. The cover sheet has a handwritten title—*The Un-Dead*—and a smudged byline that looks like it says Barn Stoker. No...it can't be that... it's Bram. Yeah, Bram. Bram Stoker. And inside is a story that's got this guy Harker visiting a mysterious nobleman in eastern Europe. Sounds kind of like the Dracula story, but this is clearly an early draft.

Donaldson's heirs had found an artifact that Dracula scholars have coveted for decades—and they decided to do the obvious thing: Sell it. Through a California book dealer, Peter Howard of Serendipity Books, they sold the typescript to John McLaughlin, owner of The Book Sail bookstore in Orange County, California, where it stayed until 2002, when McLaughlin approached Christie's of New York to auction the book off.

The Un-Dead typescript became the property of Paul G. Allen, one of the founders of Microsoft. He got it direct from Christie's, and he is only the fourth person to own it since Stoker himself scrawled the title on the cover page.

But at least part of that early draft had its origins in the Strafford Hotel on Broad Street in Philadelphia, written upside-down on hotel stationery.

WHITMAN AT 200: FACE TO FACE

Jason Koo

In 2019, we celebrate the bicentennial of the birth of Walt Whitman, a poet who nonchalantly celebrates himself at the start of his most famous poem yet now seems ironically almost impossible to celebrate. How do we do it? Where do we start? As the father of American poetry, the visionary who revolutionized English verse and transported poetry from the Old World definitively into the New? As the grammar school dropout who through his own Emersonian self-reliance published a book at his own expense that would make Emerson himself write to "greet [him] at the beginning of a great career," saying he "rubbed [his] eyes a little, to see if this sunbeam were no illusion" and that he found it "the most extraordinary piece of wit and wisdom that America ha[d] yet contributed"? As the original Brooklyn badass, the iconic hipster who published that book without his name on the cover or title page, only his casual, cocksure image on the frontispiece? As the queer, outsider poet of the margins, "one of the roughs," champion of the oppressed and disenfranchised, "the one white father" in June Jordan's estimation "who share[d] the systematic disadvantages of his heterogeneous offspring trapped inside a closet"? As the groundbreaking poet of the body, "disorderly, fleshy and sensual," giving voice to "forbidden voices…of sexes and lusts"? As the wise, timeless poet of the soul, one of the world's great mystical gurus, poet of superconsciousness whose tongue "encompass[es] worlds and volumes of worlds"?

It is a testament to Whitman that none of these celebratory appellations, or even all of them together, does him full justice. As he himself anticipates in "Song of Myself," "My final merit I refuse you," daring us,

> Encompass worlds but never try to encompass me,
> I crowd your noisiest talk by looking toward you.

In this age of *the* noisiest talk, Whitman continues calmly to evade our attempts to define him, curiously not by retreating from us but by *crowding* us, standing right before us "face to face," as he says at the start of "Crossing Brooklyn Ferry." Not by talking over us but by silently regarding us, witnessing and waiting, "curious what will come next." More than any other poet, Whitman reminds us of what is beyond mere words, "what the talkers were talking," how vital it is to be in the world face to face, not face to phone, especially the world of another human being, which houses so many worlds within it. He knew the I is always many, contradicts itself, contains multitudes, and no amount of words, even the reams that he wrote, could ever capture its deepest mysteries or approximate the life we glimpse when we look into a single human face.

> What is more subtle than this which ties me to the woman or
>   man that looks in my face?
> Which fuses me into you now, and pours my meaning into you?
>
> We understand then do we not?
> What I promis'd without mentioning it, have you not accepted?

When I think of the greatness of Whitman, what's worthiest of celebrating, it's not any particular line or passage or poem, not anything he represents, but what he promises "without mentioning it," this something staggering beyond the page, far back of the voice who speaks to us. There is this constant summoning in Whitman's greatest poems, as from a source, that leaves you dazzled, so that you end up rubbing your eyes a little at it, as Emerson did, because it does not seem altogether possible.

> Dazzling and tremendous how quick the sunrise would kill me,
> If I could not now and always send sunrise out of me.

When we look at the whole of Whitman's work, not just his massive output of poetry but his equally massive output of prose, this summoning seems even more impossible because it comes out of nowhere in 1855. Nothing in Whitman's poetry or prose before this suggests that this otherworldly eruption is coming, and so much of what comes after it is, frankly, terrible, including his endless revisions to the work, which, as Mark Doty says in "What Is the Grass?", end up "nearly ruining it," so "enchanted" was Whitman "by what had first compelled him." In fact, if this doesn't sound too strange to say after just talking up Whitman's greatness, in some ways Whitman was not even a good writer, just as he was, in some sadly glaring ways, not a good man, revealing racist views in his prose and documented conversation that make any lover of the poet cringe, if not outright reject him, and provide any critic with fodder for condemnation. As Lavelle Porter writes in an article on bicentennial celebrations of Whitman, "I submit that this is not a moment for uncritical celebration of the Poet of Democracy," and indeed when Whitman asks in "Crossing Brooklyn Ferry," "What is it, then, between us?", we can't help but hear that question a little differently from how he intended it, knowing what we know now about the sometimes striking, disappointing difference between Whitman the all-embracing poet of the people and Whitman the historical person. What would that person have thought of the poets who have followed him, his heterogeneous offspring?

Shamon Williams, a young black poet who placed third in the 18–22 age bracket of Brooklyn Poets' Whitman Bicentennial Poetry Contest, speculates on the historical difference between that person and his offspring by hearing in Whitman's question the start of a confrontation between a young black citizen and a racist police officer:

> Is it my curls?
> The strain in *Hello, Officer*?
>
> Is it my obsidian skin?
> The power in *show me your license and registration*?
>
> Is it my eyes searching for yours
> And finding their reflection in your shades?

If Whitman the poet is always "looking toward" us, welcoming us "face to face," Whitman the person often seems to have his eyes hidden by shades like the officer in Williams's poem. But this apparent contradiction lies at the heart of Whitman's creative power; he anticipates his own contradictions, objecting to them in a far more devastating way than any #cancelled tweet could muster, generating out of them a tougher, more maturely "knotted" connection:

> My great thoughts as I supposed them, were they not
>   in reality meagre?
> Nor is it you alone who know what it is to be evil,
> I am he who knew what it was to be evil,
> I too knotted the old knot of contrariety...

Whitman is always anticipating us, outflanking our understanding with his own outsize openness, tenderly amused. "What thought you have of me now," he reassures us, "I had as much of you—I laid in my stores in advance, / I consider'd long and seriously of you before you were born."

I submit it would be pretty silly of us to assume that this poet who spawned whole nations of poets, this once-in-a-cosmos consciousness, did not anticipate everything we're saying about him now with the benefit of our two-hundred years' hindsight, including our harshest criticisms, would not want a celebration of his legacy to recognize all the complications and contradictions that go right to the heart of this vexed nation itself, the one he tried so hard to embody. There is this *place* that Whitman's greatest poems come from far wider than the frame of our articulated consciousness, that crowds even his own noisiest talk; what do all his endless additions and revisions to the original *Leaves of Grass* suggest but that Whitman himself was staggered by what he had done, not knowing where it had come from and desperately trying to get back to that place? Whitman the historical person was just as much the "you" of his poems as any of us. Instead of "place" we might say "face," this serene, sublime "looking toward" us, daunting, unflappable, more rock face than human face, as Desirée Alvarez intuits about Whitman in "Primero Sueño, First Dream: On Crossing, A Whitmanesque," the third-place winner of the 23+ age bracket of the Brooklyn Poets contest. "Big rock, your lips look like ancient waves," Alvarez writes,

> Your mouth reminds me of my wife's kisses goodbye.
> I am lonely as the moon. *Por favor*, speak to me,
>   face in the grass.

Perhaps the greatest testament to Whitman is how often, how greatly his heterogeneous offspring speak back to this "face in the grass," amplifying the vision. As Ed Folsom observes, "The temptation to talk back to Walt Whitman has always been great, and poets over the years have made something of a tradition of it. There's nothing quite like it anywhere else in English or American poetry—a sustained tradition, a century old, of directly invoking or addressing another poet." We see this tradition thriving today, expanding far beyond England and the Americas to young Kelsey Wang in Taiwan, a junior at Taipei American School who placed first in the 13–17 age bracket of the Brooklyn Poets contest, who seems to sing to Whitman for all of us when she imagines how "the end was meant to be": the "kingdom of your heart, and in it, us."

WHAT IS IT, THEN, BETWEEN US?

Shamon Williams

Is it my curls?
The strain in *Hello, Officer*?

Is it my obsidian skin?
The power in *show me your license and registration*?

Is it my eyes searching for yours
and finding their reflection in your shades?

Is it the CDs, or the Skittles? The neighborhood?
The AriZona tea? The hoodie? The whistling?

Is it my negro nose? My plush lips?
The lust in *please step out of the car*?

Your braised fear of the dark?
Your nerves jittery like water disturbed?

The mugshots on the news
with **thug** slung across the screen?

The profile you pushed on me?
The paid vacation awaiting you?

Is it the blue suit or the gold badge?
The gun glinting on your belt?

Is it my unarmed hands reaching skyward?
The quiver in *please don't shoot*?

The trigger arched and wanton against your finger?
The stout *stop resisting*?

Is it the crescendo of our breathing?
Is it our genes sewn in us like flags?

Is it the cracks in the concrete gorged on blood?
Your hands hungry for my bones?

What is it, then,
between
          us?

PRIMERO SUEÑO, FIRST DREAM:
ON CROSSING, A WHITMANESQUE

Desirée Alvarez

What is it then between us?
¿Qué es entonces entre nosotros?
My horse is afraid of you and both of us are thirsty.
Stone face, we crossed the seas from Spain,
I've been riding for days past pyramids in Mexico.
Whatever it is, it avails not—distance avails not, and place avails not.
My horse and I are tired of the blistering desert.
Who is your family, crowd of great heads in a field?
Who has conquered you and whom will I now conquer?
Big rock, your lips look like ancient waves.
Your mouth reminds me of my wife's kisses goodbye.
I am lonely as the moon. *Por favor*, speak to me, face in the grass.
I remember the first time I put my fingers inside a woman
and the first time she put her fingers inside herself.
I too had receiv'd identity by my body,
my body the body uncertain, my body mixed,
dreaming of being a Spanish conquistador,
dreaming of being an Olmec head, carved and mouth sealed
forever. *Keep your places, objects than which none else is more lasting.*
We plant you permanently within us.
Being what—an across, a Zarathustra, a span
of scarf woven of seventeen colors from what roams,
what flies, what swims and what sings. Being a woman and a man,
stone-crafted and aqueous, being brown, being tree and flood-tide,
being free citizen of the body earth, electing in revolt
to expand and bring down whatever rises between us.

REDSHIFT

Kelsey Wang

I wanted to reach out, perhaps
to touch, to prove you're really there, but the distance of the earth's axis
came between us.
It's okay, if you don't want to answer.
You don't need to speak, I only want you to know...
Watch, the lovely and shattered pieces of the moon reflected in his eyes.
Spun-cotton threads of silver interwoven
like strings of fate. *It's strange, how I've*
forgiven you but I have yet to find someone willing
to do me the same.
If I had told you this then, would you
have given me your world and carved a place
for me to belong, even though it was not what I wanted?
The sky was burning softly with a strange light like blood. Prayers
swallowed and spat out all twisted and wrong.
Apologies muttered the same way.
Do not think they meant anything, sweetheart, so just
light the burning stars in the sky as if in a dream.
We're waiting, in this dream of deception and illusion, until
we meet again on a full-moon's night without the stars. You're just that sure
I'll be there with you then, right?
I'm not hoping for justice. I'm not hoping
for an explanation. If it was made to be this way,
from the start, this singular and accursed fate, this
doomed and pompous martyrdom—
then so be it. If this be the taste of our conclusion. If this is
what the end was meant to be.
The kingdom of your heart, and in it, us.

STRUCK FROM THE FLOAT
FOREVER HELD IN SOLUTION

Jason Koo

Scuzzbuckets, my thanks.
You kicked me out of comfort and showed me how
Comfort was conniving to make me content
With an almost life, the life I sort of wanted to have.
And now I'm blasted out of sort of into the sun
Tonnage of this city. Look at the Bridge accelerating against the sky, taunting
      the tourists
With their tiny cameras
On the puny pier. It dares me to think of it
As a mere amenity, though this was the life
Ever since I first read Hart Crane and saw him on the roof of 110 Columbia
      Heights
Boasting the Brooklyn Bridge as his background.
He came with nothing and left buildings.
I came, even reduced by you, with much more
And walk around his old neighborhood
Like it's my inheritance. I walk past 110 Columbia Heights,
Where a Jehovah's Witnesses building now stands.
I see through their Watchtower to Crane's Broken Tower.
Out of the rubble of his life
Just one phrase's *swift unfractioned idiom* annihilates their literature.

I look down at the gleaming musculature
Of the East River and imagine Whitman curious in the crowd on Robert
      Fulton's Ferry
Imagining me. Did he imagine me, most particular me,
The only son of Korean immigrant parents, crossing with the others on the
      ferry?
I don't think I would have occurred
To him, which is no offense, as even the Brooklyn Bridge did not occur to
      him.
You could say Roebling, and then Crane, out-imagined Whitman,
But he had the right, the original idea.
And you can still feel his presence, my enemies, in the movement of these
      waters,

The generosity of his imagination rippling to me
Not banked by its limits, the kind of generosity you did not extend to me
As you imagined my life going nowhere.
I try to extend this generosity to you, shamed by Whitman
Into questioning my enjoyment of the view
On this gentrified shore, the reward for what I've done.
I could say I'm not as bad as you think, but it's true: I'm worse than you
        think.

Whitman knew this, knew *what it was to be evil,*
How we shouldn't be fooled by any soaring, generous spirit, least of all his,
That there was always something evil in it,
Always something conquering in the creative.
That Bridge up there, Crane's connective tissue, grand Gateway to the West,
Has evil in it, so many dark patches went into it, so many lives, quite literally,
        went into it,
John Roebling killed by it, Washington Roebling crippled by it,
Confined during construction to the same room
On Columbia Heights that Crane occupied as he climbed the Bridge with his
        own construction
And was killed by it. But his name is now an aria out of it,
His dark life made it leap with more life, just as Whitman's life made Fulton's
        Ferry
More lasting than a commute
Even after the Roeblings' Bridge replaced it
With this refurbished historic pier, where Whitman's words have washed
        up
To decorate the railings.

And now I'm enjoying the sculpted shade
Reading *East Goes West* by Younghill Kang, the heroic father of Korean
        American literature
Who made his share of enemies when he left his family behind
During the Japanese occupation of Korea, first to study Western science in
        Japan
By passing himself off as Japanese, then to flee to New York
Looking for that same rebirth, that *ever-revivified life*
That Crane sought, but inexorably unfamiliar, rebuffed by realities Crane
        never had to deal with,

Scuffling through a missionary college for a year in Canada
Reading *David Copperfield* out loud to his tutor
To gain better command of English, enough to write the first novels in the
       language
By a Korean in America. Kang surely imagined me.
He would be proud, I think, to see me living as a poet in Brooklyn Heights,
A part of his legacy, reading his book.
I'm feeling all of them, Whitman, Kang, Crane, move through me,
Wondering how I got so lucky to live in a precinct of their imagination
Then remembering that it was you, my enemies, who got me here, I had to
       be a little bad
For that to happen, so much good has come of such bad
That I can't help but worry, don't worry,
Whether I deserve it, whether I'm not the worst kind of American,
Whether I'll ever do enough to return what you gave me,
Whether I'll screw this up, whether I'll ever feel like I have enough,

Whether I am enough.

WALKING WITH REZNIKOFF:
THE LEGACY OF OBJECTIVISM

Eric Greinke

I was visited by Charles Reznikoff in 1974, about two years before his death at the age of eighty-one. I was twenty-six and living with my wife of six years in a small studio apartment crammed with books, musical instruments, art supplies and a small sailboat that we used as a combination ottoman-coffee table.

Some weeks before our visit, I had been phoned by one of my old professors at Grand Valley State University to ask if I'd be willing to spend a few hours with poet Charles Reznikoff. They'd invited him to read but he would only come if he got a meeting with me. The reason Reznikoff wanted to meet was that he had a personal prophecy for me. He saw something in my work that I did not yet see for myself.

He was finally being recognized at the end of his life, but he wanted to talk to me. This still amazes me a half a century later. It took decades to understand. I had to get old myself first. At that time, I did not know who Reznikoff was nor anything about Objectivism, but he saw the path I was on.

Reznikoff and I spent several hours together prior to his evening reading, talking about poetry. He gave me four of his self-published books. He already had two of mine that he'd bought in NYC.

He was familiar with my poetry. He liked my reliance on imagery and avoidance of the first person singular. He was interested in my take on Surrealism. Although he was an older, accomplished poet, he was focused on a young beginner who had a lot to learn. I believe this alone speaks volumes about his character and his work.

At one point, we went out for a walk, and I was surprised at the gait he maintained for an old man who was also short statured. About halfway through our walk, we stopped at a small park by a pond, a few miles from my apartment. There was one other person there, a young mother with a baby in a stroller, whom Reznikoff engaged in conversation. When we resumed our walk, he told me that he'd gotten "her story." I remember this detail of our time together more clearly than our "literary" conversation. Talking the talk pales by comparison to walking the walk.

He walked an average of twenty miles a day in Brooklyn and Manhattan, observing and interacting with people. Many of his poems throughout his writing career were documentations of observations made on his long, daily walks:

> "Scared dogs looking backwards with patient eyes;
> at windows stooping old women, wrapped in shawls;
> old men, wrinkled as knuckles, on the stoops.
>
> A bitch, backbone and ribs showing in the sinuous back,
> sniffed for food, her swollen udder nearly rubbing along the
>
>   pavement.
>
> Once a toothless woman opened her door,
> showing a slice of bacon that hung from her mouth like a
>
>   tongue.
>
> This is where I walked night after night;
> this is where I walked away many years."
>
>   —from *Sunday Walks in the Suburbs*

* * *

The above excerpt is from an early work, published in 1921. The example below was written just before his death and found in his unpublished manuscripts:

> 1
> Fifth Avenue has many visitors
> and many of these have cameras;
> they take pictures of themselves, of course,
> or of buildings,
> and even of trees in Central Park.
>
> But I have yet to see anyone
> taking a photograph of the old woman
> who stands on the sidewalk
> wearing the blanket in which she has slept on a bench:
> her stockings fallen
> and showing her naked legs
> streaked with black dirt;

her grey hair disheveled
and her face also streaked with smudges.

2
The tramp with torn shoes
and clothing dirty and wrinkled—
takes a comb out of his pocket
and carefully combs his hair.

—from *Walking in New York*

* * *

Reznikoff perfected an observational, journalistic approach, transcribing actual court testimony or describing street scenes, people and things he heard. Like Whitman, he type-set and printed his own books in small editions (usually two hundred copies) on a printing press he set up in his parent's basement. Like Whitman, he evoked the poetry of common speech with the lives of common people and unadorned imagery as his subjects.

Reznikoff, in his books *Testimony* and *Holocaust* especially, used poetry to address human suffering and tyranny. He felt that images and facts *speak for themselves* without undue intrusive interpretation from the poet. Reznikoff used his experience as an attorney to write *Testimony*, which is comprised of numerous excerpts from court testimonies, with the names removed to make them symbolic of the human condition in all its permutations when dealing with legal prosecution. His immersion in studying human nature fed and energized his poetry. He had a Whitmanic, expansive ego and identified with downtrodden people across the world.

The birth of the Objectivist movement is generally seen as the publication of *An 'Objectivist' Anthology* (Zukofsky, Ed.; To Publishers; New York, New York; 1932). The anthology included the work of the precursors of the movement, Ezra Pound and William Carlos Williams, as well as the poets who later developed Objectivism. The primary poets who developed it were Charles Reznikoff, Carl Rakosi and George Oppen, along with several minor or second-generation poets (i.e., Basil Bunting, Lorine Niedecker).

Objectivism was a marriage between poetry and journalism. It has its origins in Walt Whitman, who began as a printer and was a journalist before he became a poet. Whitman integrated the objective images of America into a poetry of imagistic references that function as symbols.

The definition of Objectivism was unclear at the onset. Louis Zukofsky felt that objects themselves have immanent meanings without the artist imposing stylistic or pre-conceived interpretations on them. Reznikoff expanded that concept to include objectivity itself as the path poetry could take toward universal truths.

The Objectivists were Imagists with social and political consciences. They believed that images of human suffering and inhumanity would "speak for themselves" and cause readers to respond sympathetically. While the earlier Imagists also relied primarily on imagery, they had a meditative mental state/response more in mind, similar to the tradition of the Japanese haiku.

The early critical reception of the Objectivists was generally hostile, particularly in reviews by formalists Morris Schappes and Yvor Winters. In stark contrast to the other major poetic movement of their period (Confessionalism), the moral values of the Objectivists were humanistic while the Confessionalists were narcissistic. Unfortunately, critics and public alike jumped onto the band wagon of Confessionalism while ignoring the altruistic Objectivists. Both movements had their births in the 1930s and "peaked" in the early 1970s. Ironically, Objectivism, the less popular of the two, has left us a legacy we can build on while Confessionalism promoted a poetry of self-indulgence and sensationalism. Objectivism encouraged the belief that poetry can be a vehicle of social progress instead of (or in addition to) mere personal catharsis.

The other Objectivist poets had similar humanistic objectives with their lives and their poetry. George Oppen quit poetry for twenty-eight years in the 1930's to organize actions supporting worker's rights. He fought in WWII and was awarded a Purple Heart. He began writing poetry again in 1958. He received the Pulitzer Prize in 1969 for his book *Of Being Numerous* (New Directions, 1968).

In his introduction to Oppen's *Selected Poems* (New Directions, 2003), Robert Creeley wrote that the Objectivists "all worked from the premise that poetry is a function 'of the act of perception,' as defined by Oppen in his essay "The Mind's Own Place." Creeley continued that "Oppen is trying all his life to think the world, not only to find or enter it, or to gain a place in it, but to realize it, to figure it, to have it literally in mind." Using this definition, great similarities come immediately to mind in comparison to the theory that the microcosm reflects the macrocosm as espoused by the Transcendentalists of the previous century, Ralph Waldo Emerson, Henry David Thoreau and Walt Whitman.

Oppen speaks directly to Whitman in this excerpt from his early poem "Myself I Sing:"

> Me! he says, hand on his chest.
> Actually, his shirt.
>   And there, perhaps,
> The question.
>
> Pioneers! But trailer people?
>
> Wood box full of tools—
>   The most
>
> American. A sort of
> Shrinking
>   in themselves. A
> Less than adult: old.
>
> A pocket knife,
> A tool –
>   And I
> Here talking to the man?
>   The sky
> That dawned along the road
> And all I've been
> Is not myself? I think myself
> Is what I've seen and not myself
>
> A man marooned
>
> no longer looks for ships, imagines
> Anything on the horizon. On the beach
> The ocean ends in water. Finds a dune
> And on the beach sits near it. Two.
>
> He finds himself by two.

* * *

Like Reznikoff, much of Oppen's work is based in observations of street life that evoke humanistic concerns:

Ah these are the poor,
These are the poor—

Bergen street.

Humiliation,
Hardship...

Nor are they very good to each other;
It is not that. I want

An end to poverty
As much as anyone

For the sake of intelligence,
'The conquest of existence'—

It has been said, and is true—

And this is real pain,
Moreover. It is terrible to see the children,

The righteous little girls;
So good, they expect to be so good...

—from *Street*

* * *

The influence of William Carlos Williams on the Objectivists is clear and may be summed up succinctly in Williams most famous statement on poetics: "No ideas but in things." Williams' detached, observational approach is especially obvious in the poetry of Carl Rakosi. Like Williams, Rakosi was a master of the short, colloquial, observational poem.

Carl Rakosi also had a strong social conscience. He had a Master's degree in social work (University of Pennsylvania) and gave up writing poetry for twenty-six years in order to practice social work. After his return to the literary scene, Rakosi published several award winning collections. He lived to be one hundred years old, and is widely remembered as a kind and thoughtful man.

Although most of his poems are written in the observational first person, Carl Rakosi primarily addressed social and literary issues rather than personal ones:

> I have come to care
> for only laborers
> and poor people
> and to feel ashamed
> of poetry,
> > sitting like Chopin
> on its exquisite ass.

—from *The Dream*

* * *

In his later years he spoke directly for humanity more frequently:

> We have broken away.
> Our hearts are grounded
> in the waterways.
> Our butts foam
> in the current like a keel.

—from *Sea-Kin*

* * *

Although a limited access to the macrocosm can be achieved through literary discipline, it comes in a distant second compared to direct life experience. I believe this is why George Oppen quit writing for a long time to work directly for the welfare of workers, why Carl Rakosi quit writing to be a social worker and why Charles Reznikoff quit practicing the law to walk and write about human suffering.

The call to direct action in the world can be a strong one. I heard it myself after my first decade on the literary scene of the seventies. I had studied with Ted Berrigan and Robert Bly, and had regular one-to-one meetings with my mentor Donald Hall. I'd been published in an international anthology (*For Neruda, For Chile—An International Anthology*, Lowenfels, Ed., Beacon Press, Boston, MA, 1973). I had been published in litmags alongside recognizable names like Berge, Berrigan, Bly, Bukowski, Creeley, Felinghetti, Ginsberg, Hall, Hass, Holland, Hollo, Rukeyser, Sanchez, Stafford, Snyder, Whalen, Waldman and Yevtushenko. I'd spent three years teaching and doing workshops in the Poets in the Schools Program. I'd published my translations of Arthur Rimbaud and four poetry collections, receiving the generous support of book reviewers. I'd been Poet in Residence at two small

Michigan colleges (Ferris State and Schoolcraft). I was the poetry reviewer for the second-largest newspaper in Michigan (*The Grand Rapids Press*). I was off to a good start, yet I grew to feel that it was all so much vanity in the face of serious human suffering.

I told Donald Hall that I had a strong urge to help abused children. Don encouraged me to get a Master of Social Work degree. (His ex-wife had recently earned one, so he had direct experience of it.) "Either that, or move to New York and get serious about poetry," he said, or words to that effect. (Soon after that, Don left Michigan himself, to purchase his grandfather's Eagle Pond farm in New Hampshire. A few years ago, he wrote in a letter that he hated to leave the farm to give readings.)

I returned to school, earning a second BA, in Psychology, and then the Master of Social Work degree. For the next twenty-four years, I practiced as a therapist for special needs children and their families. Although I still wrote poetry, I didn't submit it for publication during those years. As I threw myself into trying to help children, my poetry, kept to myself, got better. I learned why I wrote it. When I returned to the literary scene, twenty-four years later, poetry had a purpose for me that went beyond the personal.

I hadn't known about the pattern of direct action among the Objectivists when I felt the call to help children. There is a special sympathetic, empathic mental space that poets enter when we focus our attention outside ourselves. I believe this state is the great potential of poetry and the ultimate legacy of the Objectivists.

In Objectivism, personal expression is limited or at least de-emphasized. However, the persona of the poet leaks through in the images chosen and described and in stylistic and tonal nuances. *Real Objectivism* is impossible, but the *self-discipline* of Objectivism is a step in the direction of greater universality. Essentially, the Objectivists were the early progenitors of universalism:

Te Deum

Not because of victories
I sing,
having none,
but for the common sunshine,
the breeze,

the largess of the spring.
Not for victory

but for the day's work done
as well as I was able;
not for a seat upon a dais
but at the common table.

—Charles Reznikoff

* * *

In an Objectivist poem, images function as universal symbols rather than as metaphors, because personal reference is absent or minimalized and images must then function at the archetypal level of the collective unconscious and its symbols. Instead of bearing a poet-assigned meaning, images used without intentional metaphors glow from the immanence of their own essential natures, where their symbolic value has been long established in human consciousness. When we focus on our commonality instead of our individual differences, we are walking the path of human progress blazed by Whitman and pursued by the Objectivists.

George Oppen expresses the Objectivist position perfectly in this excerpt from his late poem "To the Poets: To Make Much of Life:"

". . .no need to light

lamps in daylight working year

after

year the poem

discovered

in the crystal

center of the rock image

and image the transparent

present tho we speak of the abyss
of the hungry we see their feet their tired

feet in the news and mountain and valley
and sea as in universal"

* * *

The contribution of Reznikoff and of the Objectivists is highly significant because, in the final analysis, content is a higher poetic value than style. Style reflects personal values, whereas content carries a poem's meaning. Styles vary widely and are easy to come by. When considering style, we realize that even no style is a stylistic choice. There are as many styles as there are poets. Meaning, on the other hand, is always something shared with others. Sometimes a flamboyant or special style can actually obscure or hide meaning altogether, and this may be why the readership for poetry has been small. In this time of conflict and polarization, we poets need to walk the walk.

Sources

The Collected Poems of George Oppen; George Oppen; New Directions; New York, NY; 1975.

The Collected Poems of Carl Rakosi; The National Poetry Foundation; University of Maine; Orono, ME; 1986.

Holocaust; Charles Reznikoff; Black Sparrow Press; Los Angeles, California; 1975.

Poems 1918-1975, The Complete Poems of Charles Reznikoff; Seamus Cooney, Ed.; Black Sparrow Press; Santa Rosa, California; 1989.

EVEN LONERS NEED A TRIBE:
AN INTERVIEW WITH CLEVELAND WALL

Mark Danowsky: I hear your first full-length collection is about to be released! Please do tell!

Cleveland Wall: Yes! It's called *Let X=X* and it is actually here a few weeks early, after taking years and years to pull together—props to Kelsay Books for that. The title comes from the prologue poem "Proof," which takes the form of a mathematical proof of the identity X=X. It turns out there is a ton of math in my poems. But also a lot about error, which I'm surprised I admitted to so readily.

MD: Who have you been reading recently? Who do you return to?

CW: Right at the moment I'm reading a book I picked up at Caesura Poetry Festival—*The Four Ugliest Children in Christendom* by Camille-Yvette Welsch, which is poignant and funny and a bit unsettling. So really—what's not to love? Also Francesca Bell and Ross Gay. And although I have not got my mitts on it yet, I am excited about Mary Ruefle's new book, *Dunce*. The one I always come back to is Rilke. It's like wandering through this mind palace he's built and it becomes my mind palace. Strange as it is, it feels like home.

MD: You're also a musician?

CW: Ha! I am mostly not a musician, except occasional frame drum, finger cymbals, or—you know—kazoo. But I am married to a musician, which is how I also have an album coming out this fall. My husband, Michael, plays classical guitar and we perform together as The Starry Eyes, creating real-time mash-ups of poems with guitar repertoire. It's kind of an unusual collaboration in that both musical piece and poem are stand-alone works interacting with each other, as opposed to music as accompaniment. The pieces on the album, "The Garden of Terrors and Delights," are from a show by the same name, which premiered last summer at Connexions Gallery in Easton. That should be out mid-November, at least on Bandcamp. I do play finger cymbals on one of the tracks.

MD: What's the deal with No River Twice?

CW: No River Twice is an interactive, audience-driven poetry performance. It's Hayden Saunier's brain child. With her background in theater, she thought,

What if you ran a poetry reading like an improv show? So she gathered a bunch of us—there are 11 poets in our group altogether, with usually 5-6 performing in any given set—and we started playing. We each bring a book or two of our poems to work with. The first poem is selected randomly and from there the audience tells us where they want to go and we offer options. What I love about this format is that the audience is actively engaged in the performance. It makes for a more convivial mood than usual. And our styles are pretty different from each other, so you get a nice sampling.

MD: When do you find yourself coming to the page?

CW: Oh, when I'm trying to do absolutely anything else, like sleep, for example. Lines will start coming and I have to stop whatever I'm doing and scribble them down before I lose them. Then days later I'll find that scrap of paper and maybe continue the thought or maybe set it aside again and come back to it a few weeks later.

MD: What is the role of writing in your daily routine?

CW: My main practice as a poet is reading—poetry, of course, but not only that—news, fiction, essays, memes. And of course taking in all kinds of media and eavesdropping on strangers' conversations. I don't write poems every day, or even every week, but I am constantly tucking away images and little bits of info or phrases for later use. The one other consistent thing in my daily routine is my journal. I always write for a bit before bed, whether I have anything to say or not, just because the physical act of writing is soothing. Maybe that's a way of keeping the pump primed, so that thought flows almost automatically from brain to arm to pen to page.

MD: How important is music in poetics?

CW: For me, music is hugely important. That's not to say that you can't have poetic expression without it, just that I can't. Because so much of what I love in language is sound and rhythm, it would be hard for me *avoid* any assonance or internal rhyme or rhythm pattern. Nor would I want to, because that incantatory quality gives poetry a certain emotional power; it signals a shift to a different mode of understanding.

MD: Your poem "Delayed Gratification" considers a scientific experiment. Poets find inspiration from all sorts of places—are there particular areas that you draw from more often than others?

CW: I find science and math to be loaded with metaphors; also, I'm fascinated by all kinds of lore and weird news items.

MD: Many of your poems talk about bodies and often with a comical twist. We're in the year of Whitman's bicentennial and I wonder if you feel a sort of kinship with him?

CW: I do feel a kinship with Whitman. I was initially put off by his sprawling lines—like literary manspreading. How gauche! But that was more than made up for by his great heart and joie de vivre. Everything is an ode with him. I should probably praise more, but my inclination is to remain neutral.

MD: Is "Truth, Whose Clothes Were Stolen" a Me Too poem?

CW: Yes. The #MeToo movement provided this moment of stark clarity, in which women acknowledged just how bloody exhausting the harassment is and demanded accountability and then when the consequences started coming home to roost, we saw many of our male "allies"—and not a few women—close ranks around the status quo. It was kind of hilarious to see these middle-aged men watching their reputations flash before their eyes and crying "Witch hunt!" As if finally being held accountable for your actions were tantamount to being burned alive. For something you *didn't* do. I just want them to know we still see them.

MD: What advice do you have for artist-types?

CW: Find your tribe! Even I say this, inveterate loner that I am. Don't worry! You will still get to spend plenty of time all by yourself moving punctuation around. But the power of the collective is truly miraculous. For moral support, for networking, for information & resource sharing, for advice, for solidarity. Find that tribe, and be that tribe.

MD: I believe you host a series, right?

CW: My friend Elynn Alexander and I host a performance series called Tuesday Muse at the Ice House in Bethlehem—second Tuesdays when we can get them, but sometimes first Tuesday—you have to check our FaceBook page. It's mostly about creating community. We celebrate new books or albums by local & regional artists by inviting them as our featured guests and then we include open mic segments so that everyone has a chance to share what they're working on. We've been doing this since January 2019 and so far there has been at least one person at every show who is taking the stage for the first time ever, so that's pretty great. We were already fortunate to have this performance space donated by IceHouse Tonight. Now, going into our second year, we have a Project Stream Grant from the Pennsylvania Council on the Arts, through our local Lehigh Valley Arts Council, so we can offer our featured artists a modest honorarium.

Mark Danowsky is Managing Editor for the *Schuylkill Valley Journal*.

TRUTH, WHOSE CLOTHES WERE STOLEN

Truth is just a story you tell
that happens to have happened.
It doesn't have to make sense
or go anywhere. Cold facts
on a slab are hard to look at.
Oh, drape them in context.
Gauze the lens with decades.
Explain.
       Truth breathes
at the bottom of a well.
In dark and silence, she breathes.
One day she will rise
naked in the light,
and she will come for you.

BON VIVANT

Life is short.
Take the trip.
Buy the shoes.
Eat the cake.
Go ahead!
You've been good.
Treat yourself.
You can take
what you want,
so you should.
So you should!

Take the bait.
Eat the cake.
Buy the shoes—
they're a steal!
Nevermind
where they're made,
who has paid—
No big deal.
It's free trade.
You've so much
on your plate—
why not make
an escape
to some trop-
ical place
with a spa
and a gate?

If you're poor,
it's OK.
Don't be sore;
pay your fine.
Hail the chief.
Don't get sick.
Shut your mouth.
Fall in line.
Buy the shoes.
Take a hike.
Life is short.
Eat the cake.

CURED

Shoes are strung
on the telephone wire
outside the skate shop
like crutches at Lourdes,
as if their owners had been cured
of perambulation forever
and ever more would roll along
friction-free and bootless.

Appeared in *Filbert* (chapbook).

VADE MECUM

I send you, my faraway friend, this piece of slate
from the Slate Belt—smooth, a lovely pocket stone,

ideal for skipping, though you only get to do that
once. You might carry this flat, black stone

in your pocket awaiting the perfect twilight pond
upon which to skip it, meanwhile worrying it

day to day, learning its edges, its variations
of thickness, whilst thinking what to say next, how

to express what's at the corner of your mind.
Transfer it from trouser pocket to night table to next

trouser pocket. In the dark it beams back faintest
ambient light, murmuring its persistent shape

through the night. Finger it for comfort when
everything goes pear-shaped. So small, so persistent.

Carry it month after month in the city, from interior
to interior, a plausible bit of rubble amongst heaps

of rubble parceled out in tower blocks, arrived
from everywhere, artfully placed, elastic in significance.

Burnish it with finger oils and friction; steep it
in mana; consult its contours to learn the best

argument for what you already know you want.
It could be any number of seasons before you come

to the brink—it might be dawn—of a pond so still
it summons the stone from your pocket. Will you

release it? Is this what you've waited for? Imagine
your smooth, black stone leaping unstonelike

across a pool of tenuous light, grazing the surface
lightly, then less so, touching down

at ever diminishing intervals until it is vibration,
then gone, only a ructure on the pond's skin to show

where it dipped below, its perfect destiny
married to yours, after long entanglement.

Will you be reluctant to part with this stone
or will you sidearm it boldly, give a last spin

as it leaves your fingertip to speed it on its way?
You might forget by then where it came from,

its arrival a tiny detail in your long acquaintance.
If you should throw awry, imagine the fatal, solitary

plonk, the mournful ripples echoing—
all that time together for only this. Whatever

happens will be right. You've gone so far
together already and I've not even sent it yet.

Appeared in *Let X=X* (Kelsay Books, 2019).

ONCE I THOUGHT I WAS WRONG, BUT
I WAS MISTAKEN

My first pets were fish. I was keen,
named everything in the aquarium—
each fish and even the plants, Phillip and Geoffrey,
and lo! two water snails stowed away
in the foliage, a pair of gentleman callers
welcomed as accidental pets, which spawned
an infestation. Oh, but *they* were never that.
I had named them: Xavier and Ignatius.
How can a thing fall out of being once given
a name? A name will carry you
even through hell if you hold fast to it,
or so goes (blessèd, unfalsifiable) the lore.

But what of the gentle brontosaurus,
that is no more and never was?
Head of one apatosaurus, body of another,
the specious species arose not
from primordial soup but from a wishful will
to find the next big thing. We all believed
this fiction, figuring paleontologists ought to know.

And poor, demoted Pluto, once counted ninth
amongst our planets. What now of the handy
mnemonic it neatly completed? My Very Earnest Mother
Just Served Us Nine…what? Just Served Us
Nothing. Maybe I loved Pluto for its eccentricity,
skewed orbit, outlier aloofness. In retrospect,
the many anomalies should have tipped us off.
This was not one of our own stood out in left field
watching the clouds go by; it belongs to another tribe,
another class of object altogether—nothing to do with us.

Is it you I long for, my lost pets? I know you are false.
I do not love you. But I loved thinking I knew
how the stars were situated, what the bones meant,
dug up in the American west. How tiring it is
forever revising one's map of the world!
Each supplanting discovery, each step
closer to true feels more unsteady.

O my brontosaurus, my Pluto, my bonus water snails—
is it to some graveyard at the edge of town you have gone?
Are you languishing in the Kuiper belt, that junkyard
of disused forms that cool from star to rock and stand
as monuments to a lovelier reckoning of themselves?

Appeared in *Let X=X* (Kelsay Books, 2019).

PERIOD PIECE

That day when I went to the Sutro Baths with Meredith
    and her crazy boyfriend—
that boyfriend who had a death wish
    we didn't know about—
when I blithely tagged along, forgetting all about my period—
    my good, unmoody, crampless period that tended to slip
    my mind like an easy baby that doesn't fuss—
when I set out with probably the tampon from
    the night before and no spare—
that day when after our walk around the ruins
    the boyfriend suggested a hike
    along the cliff trail to Lands End—
the trail that looked dubious to start, then dwindled
    from cowpath to goat path to sparse
    series of footholds on sheer scree—
the trail we were well along when the first hot burble
    reminded me it was second-day gush and this
    was going to become untidy—
when I dared a glance down the slope at the churning
    surf and jagged rocks below and said, Will,
    I do not think this is a proper trail—
for that was the boyfriend's name—Will—we formed
    a Victorian allegorical tableau where I was
    Woman Walking the Precipice of Anatomical Destiny
    and Meredith the Sylph of Better Judgment,
    both led astray by a reckless Will—
who protested, No, no—people hike here all the time;
    there's a trailhead and everything at the other end—
when in the periphery triumphal blasts of seawater
    smashed against the larger rocks offshore—
when the scent of my own blood atomized in the salt air
    and I hoped the others couldn't smell it
    and was glad of my discreet black pants—

that day when buffeting wind filled my ears and panic
      nipped my heels and I could see no way forward
      and thought I'd perish there—
that fierce blood note buoyed me up and said,
      Not today, girl! We are not done with this world—
and Will guided me past the crisis and I came safe
      to the end of the trail, where a sign advised
      No hiking / People have fallen to their deaths—
but we hadn't and I still had the blood-clotted pants
      to deal with, which seemed a small problem
      in that deep, physical silence.

MY ROGUE SELF

All this effort to get a hold of myself
when my claim is tenuous at best.
All my waking hours I am constructing
this elaborate person with likes and dislikes,
ideas, idiosyncrasies—all very detailed
with a favorite Surgeon General's Warning,
favorite name of a chapter in a book
(Psychology and a Pound of Nuts).
I adopt foreign phrases, cherish irregular verbs,
prime numbers, buttons, night-blooming
jasmine, the subjunctive mood.
It is a very particular person I make
and gad about the world as and imagine
I can open and shut the blinds on her.

I am stunned afresh each time I find
she's been on walkabout without me,
like Gogol's Nose—or worse, not she,
the intended avatar, but some accidental other
who shrugs off my embellishments
without a backward glance, becomes
Tuesday Library Lady,
Brian's Kooky Little Sister, The One
With the Lemon Meringue Car,
Grilled Pastrami With Pepperoncini Black Coffee!
And these are just the ones I can guess
and don't mind mentioning in my poem
because they aren't terribly embarrassing,
maybe even endearing, because
I have already forgotten, already sunk
back into the comfy velveteen chaise longue
of imagining I have some say
in how this self is seen or not seen.

Meanwhile, there are hundreds
of rogue selves out there—I know it—
some of them foolish, some bad,
some scarcely connected with the original
overwrought farrago: just the physical image,
an extra in some stranger's dream.

There is no calling them back now
they're loose in the world. They carry on
like radio waves into space, distorting
very slowly dissipating, so along with the current
rogues there are old ones still roaming,
interfering with the new, making nodal lines
and their opposites, the convergence pattern
discernible only from a great distance.
The Girl With the Cat on Her Head and—
okay, yes, I know—The Heartless Ex,
The Worst Friend Ever.

But those aren't really me. At least,
not any more than my own fussy construct.
So when someone says,
"We were talking about you the other day"
I am doubly flummoxed. First because, yet again,
I can't fathom a notion of me existing
without my being there, furiously pedaling
the dynamo to run the generator to project
my own flickering, blinking figure
(walking round the garden, waving
to the camera). And then, since it's not
that mannered self, I wonder
which of the rogues is it this time?
Can I suavely like a diplomat disavow
any knowledge of her or her mission?

Probably not. The worst of it is,
these cheeky buggers, these rogues
will likely be capering about for years
after I'm gone, just as a version of
my Aunt Mary is still breathing loudly
through a mouthful of pins,
pinning a hem. I doubt it's the self
she'd have elected to survive her.
I picture them gathering over my bones
on the anniversary of my death,
all those rogues selves, and dancing
on my grave. How like them!

Previously appeared in *Schuylkill Valley Journal*.

DELAYED GRATIFICATION

In the experiment
children were given
a marshmallow each
and promised another
if they could wait.
Now tasted better
to some than *two*—
the whole pillowy mass
filling their mouths
at once, soft but resistant,
dense with couched air.
The study followed
to see who succeeded.
To no one's surprise,
the patient ones
ended up with more
in life as in the lab.
I ate my marshmallow early
and now am hungry,
but not for marshmallows.
What else have you got
behind your two-way
mirror, Doctor?

Appeared in *Transcendent Visions*.

CONFETTI

Because the ice machine was broken
and I had to go up to the next level,
bucket under my arm, because
I was parched nigh unto death,
my achy bare feet took me past
the place where three bits of confetti
winked from the hotel hallway carpet,
three penises cut
out of chrome-finished plastic—
two pink, one silver.
And my mind wandered
to the manufacture
of penis-shaped confetti, pictured
huge industrial punches punching out
sheet after sheet of pink penises,
silver penises. Chubby, cartoonish.
Someone was in charge
of designing that silhouette.
Someone (likely else) caused a die
to be made to cut the shape out.
The many replicas were
packaged and transported
to a shop and inventoried, then sold
to a bachelorette or someone just fond
of penises, and somehow strewn
on the hotel carpet like so much
profligate seed. I put these three
strays in my pocket and carried on
in search of a functioning ice machine.

Appeared in *New Purlieu Review.*

BLACK WALNUT

*You do know their roots poison everything in their paths,
don't you?*

—Melinda Rizzo

Of all the magnificent trees under whose root ball
I might lie, of all places to lose my last bits of self,
poison or no, black walnut is for me,
for I love her frondy leaves,
her circumspect bark, neither too fine
nor too rough, and good for colic.
I love her high, straight bole, how the eventual branching off
is perfect cantilever for a swing. I love
the citrus tang of her green pods, their heft in hand,
thud on the ground. I love
the muscular squirrels leaping limb to limb and
the squirrels' wile and their fierce chittering
for sovereignty. I love the obdurate
shells and their brain-shaped meat. I love
dappled shade in summer, lacy silhouettes in winter. I love
how they show where the water is: by refusing to be
anywhere else. I love the satin grain of the wood,
its raveling flow revealed at last, and even
the toxicity, the loneliness, I love.
Oh, yes, black walnut—when I have grown past old,
let me weave myself in your silken stem
bite with your acerbic green
stain the fingers of late scavengers with juglone ink
drink deep through your taproot clearest water
under bedrock, under tonnage of earth
and flimsy bone cage. I will be
a kingdom of squirrels, light-eater, shape-shifter,
murderous as life!

Appeared in *Philadelphia Stories*.

ELEVATOR

Rickety old crate rising
through warehouse space—
I know this place, the greening
brass needle slightly bent
against the dingy half-moon light.
Whinge of motor and ratchet click.
The carpet is terrible, steeped
in God knows what. The neutral
flecks of its pattern will never tell—
Like the elevator in my dreams, I say
and suddenly realize where I am:
in the dream warehouse
where all the props and sets
are stored. Somewhere below
are all those secret rooms
I've stumbled upon in houses
that were mine for the night,
those rooms full of promise
with such changeable doors.
The numbered buttons are unreadable
which only proves this is a dream.
I ride to the top floor
where a couple of extras are loitering
in the long, polished corridor.
Hands in pockets, he inspects
the sound-proof ceiling tiles.
She, in a thin dress, legs crossed,
picks her burgundy varnished nails.
They pay no mind as I slip past,
up the last steel stairs to the roof.
The white sky opens wide
and the wind picks up
under my outspread raincoat wings
and I fly away into the next scene
which I have yet to dream.
Someplace green, I tell the wind,
and drop me softly please.

EXIT SIGN

The rain has been pelting
down for days. The ground
is soaked, the cinema
too full. The windshield
dream-lapses: big dots,
little dots. An exit sign
is pointing up—but the road
doesn't go that way.

Appeared in *Filbert* (chapbook).

MERMAID

Phil Huffy

She lingers where the screenhouse may have been,
considering the lake, unchanged and still
and in the August heat remembers when
she splashed across and back with strength and skill.

Her younger self was supple, smooth and calm,
a sculpted beauty, powerful and trim,
who found the sunshine's company a balm
and thought the crossing but a pleasant swim.

Though years have not addressed the lake and shore,
the rustic camp thereby has not well fared.
The screen house isn't present anymore
and a tired fence slopes downward, unrepaired.

The mermaid now departs this hallowed place
but recollects the water's soft embrace.

WATCHING FOR MANATEES

Barbara Daniels

What is it with summer? First
everything's lit and glorious—
blooming crepe myrtle, children

in bathing suits carrying towels.
Then summer goes way too far,
murders flowers, blisters arms,

burns my sad hound of a face.
Heat runs at me with push pins.
Palm fronds wither and drop.

The childhood friend I'd mostly
forgotten for fifty years returns
in videos on the internet, her

marriage, the son who died,
her own recent funeral. I see
she was lovely all her life.

Piece-of-tin morning glares,
the sky a blue hammer
that clangs and won't stop.

What will comfort me? I hear
bird calls and turn to find
lichen formed on a tree trunk

with the precision of needlepoint.
Sudden smoothing on the surface
of water is the sign of a manatee.

In a moment its human face
will rise for the necessary breath
and then be gone in the murky water.

CENTROLENDAE

—known as the Glass Frog

Joan Colby

The glass frog exposes its heart
Pulsing with the regularity of time.

A clock of compulsion you can pray to
Like the incarnation of the Sacred Heart.

A valentine betrays the bloody fist
Appended with hoses. It is not

Divine; an esthetic error.
Surround the heart with lace and rosebuds.

With sentiment fake as vows.
The heart's imperfect design

Outweighs the vitals: stomach
And liver. Operatives of consumption

And waste. Love lives like a hermit
In the brain behind the blood barrier—

A moat that keeps you sane
When the heart accelerates.

True love as rare
As the glass frog.

A complexity of evolution
Like the transparency of language

That says *Here.*
Come here.

LOVE POEM LXIV: TURKEY

Tim Gavin

I am sitting on a busted chair in the courtyard
Of St. Matthias deep in the rural mountains once
Again agonizing when I return home,
Will I consider coming back?
Coming back to see this turkey—his right foot tethered
And the line anchored to a tent peg
And he circles, gobbling and pecking
At the line trying to free himself—
Does he wonder whether there must be more to life
Than this circumference—a limit
From one extreme to another,
Think about his own spiral of history,
His proud plumage and his snood and wattle?

Does he think of being, as he once was,
Buried in bush and brush,
Feeling secure like a bull ready
To bellow, shaking the ground
With luminous anger of his steps,
Fire on the fringe of his wings,
Leading a charge against the foreigners,
ambushing them with curiosity and dread,
Understanding he has the upper hand
And he can be brutal if he desires
Or just forget it all and call it history?
Or can he bring me back to this spot
On this broken chair where I contemplate
If it makes a difference or not—
That coming to terms with
This current radius
Is all he and I will ever know?

A POEM CAN BE A WARNING

Will Reger

In the poem I will write today
I am sitting down to write a poem.

A poem is little more than a space to put stuff,
a bullet, a flower, a mother, a prayer, bones.

Whole bodies can go here;
once I packed an entire winter in a poem.

All the weariness of a person can be stacked
here or thrown in willy-nilly through the windows.

I stand outside my poem with boxes,
barrels, a pick-up truck, and an earth mover

rumbling up with whole lives
scraped into a heap out of nothingness.

I build roads in the poem and write crowds
to line both sides of the road, shouting

protest slogans in the rain.
I walk down the middle of the road waving

or tossing garbage at the crowds
until the entire poem fills up with wet trash

and the cold rain I wept into it. When I am
weary and the poem becomes an endlessness

I can never fill—a borderless white field,
not white with snow, or white already to harvest,

but a field white with nothingness, endless
nothingness, in which I sit, a dark morose figure,

a tiny black dot containing a soul,
or the key to a soul, or the bloody first knuckle

of a soul's left pinky, left to me or by me
as a warning. A poem can be a warning.

A warning full of rain, full of white nothingness,
full of silky white seed fluff, about to blow away.

NIGHT LANDING

Don Hogle

How can you *not* believe—eyes shut,
head tilted to the last of the sun stroking
your eyelids, these two pink moons?

The bus inches down Broadway,
but you're in no rush, eyes open now
to the contents of your consciousness:
a curbside woman hesitates, shifts
her sight from one traffic light to another.
Should she cross this way or that?

Behind her, in the warm light of Starbucks'
windows, people read. There's a science
to the temperature of light—3000° Kelvin
is amber and soothes; seen from the cool
blue evening, it invites. Two rows of lights
run parallel, making a runway; they narrow
to an inevitable landing point, and then
what—a door, a window, yet another
crossing, or only night?

CARYATIDS ON A CONDEMNED BUILDING

Chris Bullard

The stone figures with arms bolted into postures
      of surrender seem bloodless as clouds.
Niche holders, plastered with white as though rolled
      in wedding cake, they prop up
the accumulated stories of a Victorian era commercial
      dreadnaught decorated like a breakfront.
Sculpted as ideal forms, their collective bearing
      defined the grace of accepted weight.
Servitude has zig-zagged their thighs with cracks.
      It's all coming down. Something sleeker
is being planned for their former lot. A billboard
      presents a glass curtain requiring no masonry
devotion, reflecting a crowd of modern-dress bystanders,
      blurry as ghosts, though free to wander.

STAGE-SET

Ray Greenblatt

The dense groves of trees
have been stored in the wings,
they'll be pushed onstage
again tomorrow.

The ocean fretful
all day churning huge teeth
somehow quiets under
cover of darkness.

Late arriving ship
nudges into harbor
its bright spotlight eye
glaring into all bedrooms

then snaps off for the night.
The actors are now at home
their roles in another dimension,
music filed in memory.

It is time to sleep
to think about today's events,
let dreams expand our lives
into Romance or Tall Tale

or even—who knows—Myth.

THE SECOND STORY

Chris Bullard

How enormous the adults appear when they come downstairs,
      staging their epic interventions.
One sings to the mirror while waving a razor as he threatens
      to take noses from the disobedient.
The other enchants with face powder, lips like a red shield
      and a perfume of tobacco and attar.
In the bedtime story they tell him, he is the prince called upon
      to slay dragons and do fantastic deeds.
The boy feels that he is only a mouse in the corner of a picture book.
      He wants to climb down the magic vine into the world,
leaving his bedroom kingdom, but the giants whisper to him,
      "It is for you that we have created this fairy tale.
If we, survivors of war and deprivation, became real for you,
      you could never escape from our tragedy."

PRACTICE

Richard Moyer

A green hill
warbling birds
—perfect target
For an artillery barrage.

THE SKY

Philadelphia, PA, July 18, 2018
For Tyree and Tyyon Bates

Luray Gross

Yesterday began in coral and gold. Pink/gray clouds flocked
the circumference of sky. What notes dawn was offering
I will never know complete, though I tried to listen.
Love, St. Paul wrote, beyond all, love.

For two years John Constable painted clouds, only clouds.
The sky, he wrote a friend, is the chief organ of sentiment.
If its notes could be heard, all else might follow.

Today, clouds shift and gather. They thin, then aggregate—
their notes too low or high for the human ear.
We know thunder—its basso proclamations,
its rumble growl. We know the keening of wind.

"I know he's coming back,"
the brother of the gunned-down 14-year old says.
"Is that like a dream?" Until now, only a year separated them,
a year and three letters in their names.

So much we do not know: how to mend what is broken,
how to claim what has been healed,
how to rightly apologize, to do a needful thing.

How is one to live? We come back to the question,
jolted or consoled by sky or sea or the depth of an eye,
the strident power of bow on strings,
of hammers hitting the keys.
Constable painted. Some of us just yearn.

Now a density of gray moves steadily east.
One can only watch and wonder.

Kubler-Ross sat by a dying girl and watched her draw a tank.
In front of it, a stick figure holding a sign that said STOP.
The doctor took the pencil, did all she could:
she drew another person steadying that child.

I spend hours looking at an immensity of sky:
troposphere . . . mesosphere . . .exosphere . . .
Sometimes it is too difficult to look down.
Impossible, it seems, to hold that child's hand.

AMISH ELEMENTARY SCHOOL MASSACRE

*Females between the ages of six and 13 were shot execution style
and fatally wounded.*

—CBS-3 News, 10/2/06

Edwin Romond

The coroner had to stop,
said she could not continue

after charting the twenty-fourth
bullet in the six year old

girl from the one room
Amish school. They'd just finished

recess, maybe they played tag,
and no one wanted to be "it."

Charles Roberts told the girls
he was angry with God, then

aimed his gun. Perhaps Satan
saves words in hell's

dictionary to describe
little girl after little girl

overcome with terror and lead
dropping to the floor

in dresses stitched
by mothers who'd be brought

to the morgue to identify
their daughters, who'd stand

beside a pulled back sheet
and whisper, "She is mine."

LOST CHILD

Joseph Cilluffo

I remember the child I never knew,
the one who, like the sea in a shell,

beat with a borrowed heart.
Our first child, sexless as the salt

we'll never reclaim from the sea.
The child who we never named,

whose name we maybe gave away.
This is the child we say we *lost*

—as if misplaced somewhere—
lost like innocence or car keys,

virginity, or time.

My tears for that child
were a tribute paid in a temple,

each drop was a coin
placed in the open palm of a statue,

divinity distant in its love.
I wept wheat to place at the feet

of clay-formed ancestral idols
then burn. I cried alone,

I left you alone to cry.
I was being strong for you, strong

and silent as stone.

HAIKUS

Fereshteh Sholevar

His mother's sad eyes
Watch him through the water-lilies
Her chair is empty.

Colors fall off flowers
Sparrows pack their seeds and leave
Gardens fall asleep.

He watches fireflies
The sea laments from far off
His dreams slip away.

Crickets mourn till dawn
Dews pour down his blurry eyes
Her shadow on wall.

Orphan boy at sea
Calls his mother among waves
Cruel autumn winds.

A water-lily floats
With a lit candle in its heart
In her memory.

THIRD-QUARTER MOON

—for my friend, Sandy

Marie Kane

This late November night announces itself
as Indian Summer—70° at eleven PM.
The wind almost takes the front door
when I open it to view the massive oak

across the street fling itself crazy in windy
warmth. Fall has turned its heel, pivoted back
to summer. Yet wintertime's ice and snow—
January's queen—will soon force branches

to the ground in homage to her. How pleased
she will be when they *snap*—something you
could not bear. I've convinced myself that's why
you left us in November—to not endure winter's

madness, the loneliness of snow-covered,
indifferent roads. Surprising frost glazed
the ground earlier this fall, predicting, you said,
winter's grim damage. What no one realized:

your certainty that no crocus nor snowdrop
slept beneath your landscape. No anticipation
of spring's melt since no flowers would climb
toward light to fold open purple and white.

So I shouldn't be surprised that you guaranteed
winter would not touch you. Later that evening,
the third-quarter moon rose, its left side bright
with reflected sunlight.

PRAYER LISTS

R. A. Allen

It used to be,
I want, I need, I must have.
Ad hoc appeals to God:
let that traffic light
stay green till I get through;
keep her in slumber
when I stumble in late;
and for more money, of course.

Notes of anxiety
crept in at midlife:
one prayer for take-offs,
another for landings,
a few more to win this last woman,
and then fresh ones to keep her.

But for now, please gently explain
this newfound wheezing,
this frightful forgetfulness,
this lump.

And when our words are drying up
our greed for life will cry out only
to see the light of one more sun.

APRICOTS

Vasiliki Katsarou

They stand frozen
in the family backyard
not too tall, not too short

two teenagers stranded
one from the other

apricot trees
planted by my father
to remind him of faraway home

the bitterness of waiting
for that yearly handful
of hard green knobs

and why it was rarely the sweetness of fruit,
the velvet cheek in his hand,
juice dripping down the chins

Were they the same
sex? Did the bees avoid them?

eventually blossoms appeared
but the ripening always evaded
his impatience

Did he rue the work?

*

Apricot-scented sense of waste-not
want-not

he'd say he was "all used up"
by the time he turned forty,

and so I was born,
first fruit of his later used-up years

now he's gone
left the apricot trees to stand alone
in every season

      as all that sweetness
drip,
      drip,
            drips
onto a velvet floor.

I TAKE MY FATHER FOR HIS LAST HAIRCUT

Joseph Cilluffo

Although, of course, we don't know yet that's what this is
—the doctors say you have months left, half a year,

maybe more. The barber billows a white sheet
across your chest with a flourish

like a footman in some manor setting the table with silk.
He secures it in place, takes his silver scissors

and smiles. *What'll it be today?* After a moment
that is too long I answer for you.

Nothing too fancy, I know,
for a man always more concerned with substance.

You lived neat as a stoic, clean-shaven as Cato,
the way Christ says a man who is fasting should.

An old-school Italian, always proper
in your dark suits and the white, starched shirts

that we don't dress you in anymore.
I watch the barber wet your hair,

comb it, gently tilt your head
until you're looking into the distance,

through the ceiling, and as he combs
and cuts, the scissor is the only one speaking,

a voice as hoarse as yours has grown.
I stare at you, knowing you won't notice,

trying to memorize everything.
The eagle nose that could have belonged

on one of the Roman coins you collected.
Your brown eyes, which once were so dark

a stranger might have said that they're black,
now are milky white when the pupils don't swallow them.

I need to remember it all, but of course it's too late
—the time to pay attention is long gone.

Too quickly, it's over. Another flourish of the sheet.
A brush of talc across your pallid face.

I can tell you want to sleep. It's 2 pm.
There will be other days, so I suppose. Other chores.

If I had known this was your last haircut, the first
of so many last things for you

      — last time you'll leave the hospice,
      last time you eat solid food,

      your final words—*I love you, too*—
      my last chance to ask you

      or tell you … oh, so many things that I don't.

Dad, if I had known,

I would have swept up a lock when no one saw,
would have kept it

if I had known
I couldn't keep you much longer.

Gray hair lies on the floor around you
like—I want to say—a seated king's robes.

But really it's just hair,
haloed around you, color of ash.

No one pays it any mind
and by evening it will be swept away.

STACKING WOOD WITH MY SON

Joseph Cilluffo

We form a chain, he and I
from the pile on our driveway
to the place tucked neatly against our house
where we begin to stack the wood.
Fifteen, he doesn't need my love
like he used to. This is good,
and sometimes breaks my heart.
What else can I teach him,
old dog that I am?
I bend, choose a log
and hand it to him, watch
as he studies a moment the stack,
finds the right spot to rest it,
puzzling where to place the next.
He is building a wall.

Maybe when the stacking is done
we will choose a few logs
and I can show him how to split wood.
To take the ones too big, find their seam,
to place the wedge
where the wood already wants to part.
To strike it hard but true, with care
—so much of life
is learning not to hit your own hand.

What else can I teach him?
I suppose there's this lesson,
taught, as the best are, in what we do.
I lift a log, pass it to him,
and give thanks to God
for the wood we stack, which cost $200.
For my job, which provided the money.
I give thanks for this clarion day,
which we have no right to expect in December
but allows us to keep the wood dry,
cover it tight with a tarp, ready to warm us.
I give thanks to the Lord for my son,
who doesn't need me like he used to
but smiles as he turns with open arms
to receive the next log I hand him.

DAUGHTER AFTER A DETAIL

> *after Anthony Van Dyck's* James, Seventh Earl of Derby,
> His Lady and Child

Vasiliki Katsarou

Her plaited hands
her dress is lava
what hardens and is hidden
in a lace apron
in lace like ice, like frost, like flakes

her eyes hold a secret
her pearls are precious,
mouthless teeth ground down to perfection

her mother is satin, is silk,
is static, a guide for hiding
her own self-
making

the daughter is lava
molten fire forms her skirts
she skirts flaming mire
keeps her head above the fire

her lips will unpurse
in time.

ENVOY TO A COMING GRANDDAUGHTER

John Timpane

Little life, igniting light, you and your mother
Orbit each other. For you there's not yet any
Other, but father is there to make a

Together. Hover, gather us, nearly-here
Heart. Farther and farther in sun-tethered
Neighborhood, smothered in our nursemaid,

Nothing, we swing in a flat, round
Loop, lost as we can be. I would rather
You, yes I would; I would rather you came,

Mouther, bather, breather, soother and
Centerer, sent to us, naked in this, the
Altogether. Alter the weather within. In

Our oval wandering through the turbulent
Empty, can wonder ever be over once
You're here? We can wait. Make us better.

GOLDEN HOUR

John Wojtowicz

I pull over at Dinosaur Land
happy to find a tourist trap
with a public restroom and cheap coffee.

A decaying fiberglass blue whale
greets us at the entrance.

My daughter poses for a photo in its mouth.

We've arrived at golden hour
so even my hastily snapped pictures
look professionally polished.

She smiles big and hugs the leg
of a twenty-two foot Giganotosaurus
eating a Pteranodon.
Then runs to pat the head of an *adorable*
Velociraptor and squishes her face
against the cheek of a discolored Hadrosaurus

when I tell her it's New Jersey's state dinosaur.

She's nervous as we climb a small ladder
to stand in the weatherworn hand
of King Kong.

I squeeze her trembling one
and a gift shop clerk on her smoke break
takes a photo for us.

As the sun sets on the Mesozoic era,
she buckles back into her car seat
and sleepily kisses my cheek.

I empathize with the craggy
stegosaurus, frozen in time,
futilely trying to protect his offspring

against the Tyrannosaurus Rex of the world.

SKATERS

John Timpane

A town sleeps by a frozen lake
A single skater makes her own
With practice, practice, turn and brake
And leap. She is, she thinks, alone
But there's a doubled soloist
Beneath her blades: the mirrored one
Who shares each move and can't exist

And looks up—3-turns, change-foot spin,
Y-spiral, Axel, Chocktaw, splits—
But can't break out and can't break in.
A Salchow—and she misses it, sits
Down hard. Chagrin and bottom burn.
She gets up. Cold reflection—it's
Her eyes she sees. Turn after turn,

Her skating, in a whispered scrawl,
Defiles the mirror of the lake:
Two girls: one in an icy caul
And one of light, intent to take
That jump she landed yesterday.
She tries and falls. One more mistake
To memorize and skate away.

In gray depths, she can see the girl,
Made in her image in the ice,
Who does what she does, twirls each twirl
As she does, doubles artifice
And error. *Today is not the day,*
She thinks, and does each spiral twice,
Avoiding what she comes to say

Through the white slashes on her face:
Tomorrow, she could lose to that
Ukrainian girl. And second place.

The ice-girl leaves unspoken: *What*
Is that pain next to this?: You are,
I'm not, except in your light, caught
Shadow, forever unaware.

Two girls bend backward. Backward B
For both of her. Her mirror sky,
Her mirrored sky. It fits that she
Should make a B. Being is why
She skates in nameless sorrow. When
One girl is, and one can't be,
Two girls write once and write again.

Blunted, the sharp competitor
Works to peak before the meet
So she ignores the other her
Across the rapiered surface, fleet
In skates that edge hers, poised on cut
Meniscus-ice. The thought *defeat*,
Ajar in space … she kicks it shut.

Breath clouds, sweat steams off. What do they
Say, words she backwards-carves in ice
With eyelash tracery? They say
The skater you see, you see twice
And while she skates, keen to immerse
Herself in grace, beneath her lies
Her sister skater in reverse

Of what she thinks. The self she has
She does not own; the jump she made
Last time waits unmade. Winning was
A dream, for her and for her shade,
Whose hand flies up as hers flies down
One frozen fearless, one afraid
The surface gives way, skaters drown.

TRUE BLUE AND FALSE BLUE AND BLUE IN-BETWEEN

Luray Gross

In sleep, I reach for the girl who has not yet discerned
her pink labia or tendered her own unbudded breasts,
the girl who loves cats and singing.
When she is found chained to the bed,
those next door will claim they know nothing,
but my dream draws near to her center,
widens to touch her fingertips, her toes.
The dream yearns for a boat she can row
toward another shore.

Awake, I tell you my brain is filled with cotton.
Weave it, you say. The finest gauze for her wound,
dimity to curtain her windows, a spread of chintz
sprinkled with purple violets.
Weave sateen to ease her pain.

Let her look in the mirror and tell herself, *tonight*,
then fold the three dresses of fairy tale so tight
they snug into a walnut shell: one golden,
one silver, one that glints like a star.
"There," she will say, and tuck the walnut into her pocket,
pull on her boots, her hat, her coat with the crimson hood,
and let herself out into the night.

Perhaps she will die, she will think,
holding in her fist a thought so strange,
death being the country of the old or the sick, of the boy
who no longer sat at his desk in the row by the window,
the boy with hair like straw.

For now, she will keep walking, and I,
weaving her story out of vapor and forgetting, will wait
while the night fills with snow.

AN ARTIST PAINTS SNOW AT 3:00 AM

Marie Kane

On the dark wetness of the studio floor, an upright
        freezer with rusty hinges holds snow, snow,
snow that translates its sky-pouring calm onto his canvas.
        For reality's sake, he opens the freezer, scoops

a fist of snow, fingers flinching from its cold, almost gritty,
        texture—the snowball holds the indent of his fingers.
His palette, brushes, and brandy glass with still vigorous
        scent flank his painting of the winter pond.

Flat snow holds hints of purple and in the wagon wheel's
        gouge, deep snow-pockets reflect the moon's silver-
grey. He captures snow's tugging charcoal base, its primal
        relationship to water.

On the canvas, snow conceals the pond's gray-blue ice,
        coats branches of ghostly sycamores. Open moon-
light pours on the snow surrounding the pond that he paints
        as translucent as Carrera marble.

GENTLEMEN PREFER BLONDES AND STEAK SANDWICHES

Matilda Schieren

To be a natural-born brunette means to live under a subtle, persistent veil of inferiority. This isn't a pity cry or even a complaint, but simple fact.

- **Exhibit A**: "If only my head looked more like a Snickers bar, one-note brown with maybe some caramel low-lights for good measure," said no natural blonde scrolling through her selfie portfolio, ever.

  Famous natural blondes (I'm looking at you Emma Stone and Laura Prepon) may go five-alarm fire red in the name of *brand-building* or a specific role, but they don't go brunette. You know what Hollywood makes brunettes do to land roles? Shave their heads. Natalie Portman, Demi Moore and Robin Tunney are goddesses among mortals.

- **Exhibit B**: As an adolescent or post-adolescent Jewish female, the inferiority complex is reinforced threefold. Your head is one in a sea of infinite darkness. If your bloodline skews Ashkenazi, you're most likely pale – and that contrast only underscores the blandness framing your face. This is why ladies of the tribe are so quick to embrace the bottle (of developer). In certain pockets of certain upper-class neighborhoods, dying your God-given strands into hay is *the* rite of passage from girlie to Jewess in training.

- **Exhibit C**: I came of age in the nineties and early aughts, which means that all of the daydreams I've had about falling in love and/or performing a bold rendition of "Born to Run" in front of a large audience are a reflection of the pedestal upon which I place pop culture narratives. And if you look across the pop culture canon from my formative years, you'll find that The Makeover Motif is heavily skewed toward women with dark locks.

Mia Thermopolous, Princess of Genovia and arguably Anne Hathaway's most successful screen appearance, morphs from frizzy pyramid-topped nerd to A+ blow-out royalty. (Thus becoming an apt foil to the villainous Mandy Moore and her honey tresses.) At least one brunette on every OG season of "America's Next Top Model" gets Tyra's extreme platinum treatment (double-whammy when they go blonde and get served the Mia Farrow/Rosemary's Baby pixie.)

By the time I was 18, a college freshman and still beholden to a brown mop, my blonde ambitions were hyperactive. I was high off the rare, newfound liberty of living outside my parents' bubble for the first time in my life. I was free to eat breakfast cereal that wasn't a shade of beige ... and make it my dessert course for every meal. Free to roam around with friends late into the night, off campus, even if just a mile down the road for ice cream.

So when Chris and Claire, my two closest high school friends and first and only couples therapy patients, made the pilgrimage from South Jersey to Villanova for an impromptu visit, the stage was set for rash decisions.

The afternoon began harmlessly enough. That's to say, a continuation of everything we did in high school: walk around, find the nearest coffee shop to bicker in, smoke filtered cigarettes. And then we found our way into CVS.

Drug stores, the most innocuous form of retail, become playgrounds rampant with risk, opportunity and instant gratification between the ages of 13 and 21. When you're an 18 year-old girl in a drug store with your best friends, vibrating from caffeine and nicotine, buying a box of L'Oreal Preference in some God-forsaken shade like "golden natural blonde" seems like sweet, rebellious, reasonably priced destiny.

So I forked over the $9—or rather, paid with my preloaded Wildcard rather than my debit to throw my parents off the scent of polyglyceryl—and we decamped to the third floor of Katherine Hall.

A 200 square foot, fluorescently lit cinderblock room adorned in movie art postcards and Target's grooviest dormwear was not the makeover setting I may have dreamt at 15, but it was the makeover setting we had. Sitting in my wood standard-issue desk chair in front of a floor length, back of door mirror, I watched Claire meticulously douse my head. My roommate strolled in at some point (an oddity considering she napped through most things, including normal meal times and fire drills) and we waited.

Word travelled quickly around the women's floor, and by dinnertime a gaggle of neighbors had assembled in a friend's room waiting for the big reveal. This was starting to feel more like the daydream.

After a quick rinse and blowdry, the new me was fully realized. She wasn't as severely platinum as a Gwen Stefani or a Debbie Harry or a 2017-ish Kim Kardashian. To be perfectly honest, she was much more ... ochre, than anything else. But she was new and unfamiliar and at 18 years old I had no choice but to own it.

The women of the third floor oohed and cooed over my copper head. I won't even begin to pretend that the loving attention didn't feel good to someone who had gained the freshman 15 in the first semester alone (and would rack up another 10 before the year was up). Even hearing Wayne, the second or third object of my freshman affection, call me Gerard (as in lead singer of My Chemical Romance who went platinum around the third record) as I strolled through the business school building felt like bliss.

A few weeks later, with my roots starting to seep out, the thrill of strolling across campus as a newly minted blonde gave way to increasing anxiety.

Spring break was near. My dad, the parent who would admonish me (by way of my mom) for wearing red lipstick to high school, would be collecting me soon enough for the two-hour trek back to South Jersey, and now ritual pit stop at Dalessandro's for steak sandwiches.

In true Jewish parent fashion, he was early. Tromping back to my dorm after the last class before break, I could see the Chevy Impala from yards away. My footsteps and heart palpitations fell in lockstep. I likely contemplated taking a hard right and flouncing myself onto the high-speed rail tracks that bisected campus.

The closer I got, the more I realized that my neurosis was, momentarily, unwarranted. As my dad registered that the short girl with banana boat hair was his blue-eyed, 5'2" progeny, his Philadelphia Smile Contest-winning grin emerged. "Ya went blonde!" he said and giggled, while bear-hugging me.

Days on end of neurosis and dread amounted to literally nothing. (A few months later, after only one quick and dirty reapplication of boxed dye, there was an inevitable meltdown over the brass helmet my head had become.) But for this afternoon, all was fine—fortunately for me, because lingering panic would have cramped my favorite pre-break routine.

The drive from campus back to South Jersey was rarely more than two hours, but my parents and I had become accustomed to stopping less than 20 minutes into the eastbound trek for steak sandwiches. You're probably thinking that last line was a mistake because, you'd assume, any sandwich consumed in and around the Philadelphia city limits by law is blanketed with cheese (regardless of where it falls on the natural to artificial spectrum).

Well, yous guys are wrong.

Dalessandro's, a small shop in a residential area miles north of the art museum steps, and even farther from Pat's and Geno's warring neon signs, is where my dad and I opted exclusively for steak sandwiches. What their sandwich lacks in dairy it compensates for in width, length and girth. It's the East Coast roll you know fighting to corral heaps of chopped ribeye and onions in a volume you never thought possible on Passyunk Avenue. It needs nothing, but can easily accommodate streaks of ketchup or exceptionally fiery crushed peppers. It's absolutely the wrong thing to eat before sitting in the car for an hour and a half drive down the shore, and the only thing that feels right after holding your breath for days in nervous anticipation.

* * *

Hair grows out. Soon enough I was back to brunette, ignorant of the short window of time I'd have left with a head unadulterated by gray. Since my freshman year episode I've had no urge to dye my hair anything, outside of a vow to—once middle aged and completely gray—pursue a tasteful pastel pink.

Most brunettes have to dabble as blondes the same way that most eaters choose to cross paths with a cheesesteak. If we didn't, we'd never appreciate how satisfying the unassuming option could be.

FEMALE SERIAL KILLERS

Joe Tyson

At last count men perpetrated 89.5% of America's murders, women the remaining 10.5%. Thus, the term "serial killer" generally brings to mind males such as Jack the Ripper, Ted Bundy, John Wayne Gacy, Jeffrey Dahmer, etc. Although women commit significantly fewer homicides than men, female serial killers are out there.

Mary Ann Cotton, a coal miner's daughter from Durham, England (born 1832), slew at least twenty-one people, including her mother, best friend, four husbands, twelve children, and a lover. She was hanged on March 24, 1873.

Between 1863 and 1895 English "nanny" Amelia Dyer took in orphans for money. Most of them died from asphyxiation, poisoning, or starvation. Police suspected her of killing over four hundred children. Dyer was hanged at Newgate Prison on June 10, 1896.

Jane Toppan emigrated from Ireland to Boston as a child. A rogue nurse who derived perverse gratification from killing, she poisoned patients, landlords, friends, and her foster sister. Jane confessed to murdering thirty-one people. In 1902 a Massachusetts court ruled her criminally insane. Toppan was incarcerated at Taunton Mental Institution, where she died in 1938 at the age of 81.

Perpetually smiling Nannie Hazel Doss from Anniston, Alabama seemed pleasant and charming to the casual observer, but she poisoned at least eleven people from 1925 to 1954. An alcoholic, chain-smoker, and avid fan of romance magazines, this self-styled southern belle snuffed out the lives of four (out of five) husbands, two children, two sisters, a grandson, one mother-in-law, and her own mother. She killed second husband Frank Harrelson by adding rat poison to his moonshine on August 15, 1945. Fifty-nine-year-old Nannie died of leukemia in Oklahoma State Penitentiary on June 2, 1965.

Mary Ann Cotton, Amelia Dyer, Jane Toppan, and Nannie Doss renounced women's caretaking role. Among their victims were parents, husbands, siblings, and children, whom they viewed as annoying.

Aileen Wuornos fit a different pattern. While working as a prostitute in Florida between 1989 and 1990 she shot seven "johns" to death with a pistol at close range. Like many homicidal females, Wuornos had been sexually abused as a child. She said that her alcoholic maternal grandfather and one of his friends repeatedly molested her. In March, 1971 at age fifteen Aileen became pregnant and delivered a baby boy who was put up for adoption.

Submitting to males as a prostitute evidently triggered flashbacks in Wuornos' mind. She admitted murdering customers, but claimed to have acted in self-defense against strangers who were trying to rape her. A jury found her guilty. The State of Florida executed Wuornos in October, 2002.

Aileen Wuornos' criminal profile resembled that of Valerie Solanas, the mad feminist born and raised in Ventnor, NJ, who shot pop artist Andy Warhol through his torso and art critic Mario Amaya in the buttocks on June 3, 1968. Although she cannot be classified as a serial killer, Solanas nearly murdered Warhol, whose heart had to be restarted on the operating table. Thereafter, he had to wear a wire-mesh undershirt to keep his guts in place. Andy suffered from Post Traumatic Stress Disorder for the rest of his life, and died at age 58 from lingering effects of the bullet wound. Valerie would have fatally shot Warhol's secretary Fred Hughes in the head from a distance of two feet if her pistol hadn't jammed. While in prison she continued her hobby of sending death threats to imagined "enemies," such as Warhol, publisher Maurice Girodias, Grove Press C.E.O. Barney Rosset, and women's rights activists Robin Morgan and Jill Johnstone. Solanas accused all those individuals of stealing her literary works.

Valerie alleged that father Louis Solanas sexually assaulted her as a young girl—an accusation that her mother, sister, and cousins disputed. Like Aileen Wuornos, Valerie came from a family plagued by mental illness, used illegal drugs, gave birth to illegitimate children in her teens, carried on lesbian affairs, earned money as a prostitute, and engaged in violence against men. In 1967 she wrote *SCUM Manifesto*, a pamphlet which advocated the extermination of the male gender in order to reduce crime and inaugurate an all-female utopia. (Perhaps in this brave new world there will be robots capable of mowing grass and taking out the garbage.) *SCUM Manifesto* remains a cult classic among third-wave feminists.

Two of the heavier hitters in the female serial killers' hall of infamy are Elizabeth of Bathory and Belle Gunness.

From 1585 to 1609 Transylvanian noblewoman Elizabeth of Bathory and her sadistic minions murdered approximately 650 girls and young women.

She mainly used female procurers to recruit victims from Hungary, Slovakia, and Transylvania. Those agents promised peasant girls well-paying jobs in Bathory's Castle, located near Trenci in present-day Slovakia. They also lured daughters of lesser nobles with the prospect of free instruction in languages and court manners. (Elizabeth spoke Hungarian, Latin, Greek, and German.) Before killing victims, she and her assistants tortured them by burning, mutilation, starvation, freezing, and stabbing with needles.

Rumors of Bathory's atrocities spread throughout the region.In 1603 Lutheran minister Istvan Magyary registered a formal complaint against her in Vienna's High Court. Because of her family's political clout, the ensuing investigation took years to complete. Imperial constables finally arrested the countess on December 30, 1610. Over 300 witnesses delivered testimony against her at two trials held in January, 1611. The court found Elizabeth guilty. Due to the Bathory family's influence she was not executed, but confined to a bricked-up suite inside Cachtice Castle, without servants or visitors. She died there on August 21, 1614.

Belle Sorenson Gunness was born Brynhild Poulsdatter Storseth in Selbu, Norway, on November 22, 1859, the youngest of eight children. Her father Paul worked as a farmer and stonemason. An oft-repeated story related that pregnant 17-year-old Belle went to a country dance. At this event a wealthy landowner's son viciously beat her, causing a miscarriage. Relatives asserted that she consequently suffered a nervous breakdown, which transformed her into a sociopath.

Belle sailed to America in 1881. A large-framed woman, standing more than six feet tall and weighing over two hundred and fifty pounds, she would kill at least thirty-four people, including two husbands, seven children, a servant or two, and twenty-some male suitors.

Belle married Chicago security guard Mads Anton Sorenson in 1884. The couple had two children, Caroline and Axel. Both died of acute colitis—probably due to strychnine poisoning. After their deaths, she and Mads adopted three girls from Chicago's Norwegian Orphanage: Jennie, Myrtle, and Lucy.

Belle made a fortune through insurance fraud. In June, 1900 she torched husband Mads Sorenson's unsuccessful candy store, and collected from his fire insurance company. Then she poisoned him and received life insurance proceeds of $8,500 (the equivalent of $235,000 today). With that money she bought a farm on McClung Road in La Porte, Indiana. Within a year, the carriage house on that property mysteriously burned down, providing more insurance money.

Norse amazon Belle possessed the strength of a brawny man. Strenuous manual labor never fazed her. On April 1, 1902 she married butcher Peter Gunness, who taught her his trade. That knowledge would soon be utilized to slaughter victims. Recent widower Peter brought two children into the household. His baby girl quickly died of colic under suspicious circumstances. Older daughter Swanhilde only survived into adulthood because Uncle August Sorenson, who distrusted Belle, decided to adopt her.

In December, 1902 Peter Gunness died in a freak accident. The coroner determined cause of death to be blunt force trauma to his cranium and recommended an autopsy. Belle stated under oath that Peter's meat grinder fell off a shelf and struck him on the head. Her crying act in court induced a grand jury to believe that tale. So there was no autopsy or indictment. Belle soon received a check for $4,000 ($110,000 in 2018 dollars) as the beneficiary of her late husband's life insurance policy.

Daughter Jennie confided to a classmate, "Mama killed papa with a meat cleaver, but don't tell a soul." A few weeks later Jennie stopped attending school. Belle explained that she sent her to a Lutheran academy in California. (In the summer of 1908 a work crew hired by police dug up Jennie's remains near the farm's hog pen.)

Between 1904 and 1907 Belle managed to attract a score of lovelorn bachelors with a classified advertisement in *The Skandinaven* newspaper which characterized herself as a "comely" and affluent widow. Her pitch ended with the sentence: "Triflers need not apply." Most of the hopeful lonely-hearts who answered this ad were dispatched to the afterlife with an ax-blow to the head.

Belle invented lies when townsfolk asked about her male callers. She told neighbors that Ole Budsberg went to Oregon, Olaf Lindbloe departed in order to see the St. Louis World's Fair, and Henry Gurholt left with a horse trader. The bodies of all three men were eventually disinterred from the pock-marked lot next to Belle's pig pen.

One swain slipped out of her clutches, and subsequently provided a firsthand account to investigators. Norwegian immigrant George Anderson of Tarkio, Missouri responded to Belle's advertisement. She fed him a hearty dinner, along with a cup of weird-tasting coffee, which he didn't finish. During the meal Belle kept badgering him about whether he had the $1,000 required to pay off her mortgage. George replied to his glowering hostess that he'd only brought $300.

That night Anderson was awakened around 2 A.M. by shuffling in his room. To his shock, he saw Belle, with a "strange and sinister expression on her face," looming over him. In her left hand she held a flickering candle; in her right, what looked like a hatchet. When Anderson sat up in bed, Belle scurried out of the room. Thoroughly alarmed, George got dressed, packed his satchel, and power-walked to La Porte's train station.

Belle hired thirty year old handyman Ray Lamphere in the spring of 1907. They were soon promenading around town arm-in-arm. Initially, Mrs. Gunness showered her young lover with gifts: watches, rings, boots, a fancy vest, and beaver hat. Observant residents recalled seeing those articles before, worn by other men.

This romance ended with the arrival of South Dakotan Andrew Hegelein in January, 1908. Still obsessed with Belle, Ray Lamphere became jealous of Hegelein. He argued with her. Belle fired Ray on February 3, 1908, ordered him off her property, and refused to pay his back wages.

Andrew Hegelein disappeared in March, 1908. Four months later police unearthed separate flour and potato sacks on Belle's property which contained his severed body parts. Chemists detected strychnine in what was left of his alimentary canal.

In April, 1908 Asle Hegelein, Andrew's brother, arrived in La Porte to investigate. After hearing of his mission, Belle planned her getaway. Part of her exit strategy was to frame Ray Lamphere. She notified police that he continued to trespass on the farm and harass her. Belle demanded a sanity hearing for him. La Porte authorities did conduct one, which pronounced Ray of sound mind, despite his fondness for liquor.

New hired hand Joe Maxson remembered one of his first jobs for Belle.She ordered him to fill in several depressions on land near her hog pen. Mrs. Gunness told Joe that rain had washed away topsoil in spots where she'd buried rubbish.

Belle's complaints to police implicated Ray Lamphere as the fall guy for crimes she planned to commit. On April 27, 1908 she went into town, informed attorney M. E. Leliere of Ray's "death threats," and dictated her last will and testament, naming Myrtle, Lucy, and Phillip (her son by Peter Gunness) as heirs.

Around 3:45 A.M. on April 28, 1908 Belle, or an accomplice, set fire to her farmhouse. Hired man Joe Maxson managed to escape from his room, but Myrtle (11), Lucy (9), and Phillip (5) perished. After leaping from a second floor window, Maxson tried to rouse the children by banging on doors and windows. However, not one of them woke up in spite of the racket he made. Pathology tests subsequently confirmed that they all had strychnine in their stomachs, and were dead before the blaze started.

The managers of two La Porte banks advised police that Belle withdrew all her savings shortly before the fire. The balances in those accounts amounted to $40,000 (close to one million dollars today).

Detectives discovered a headless female body in the charred debris where the farmhouse used to be. It was not Belle, but that of a much smaller lady, 5' 3", weighing 145 pounds. The coroner's office sent detectives to clothing stores patronized by Belle. One shop recorded that she stood 6'1" tall and had measurements of 48"- 37"- 54".

A Chicago laboratory tested the dead woman's stomach and found strychnine present. Five witnesses testified that the headless female corpse in La Porte's morgue was not Belle. Neighbor John Anderson stated under oath that, a day or two before the fire, he'd seen Mrs. Gunness driving her buggy with an unknown lady sitting next to her.

Police arrested Ray Lamphere for arson and murder. He claimed that Belle had enticed the deceased woman from Chicago by offering her a housekeeping job. After poisoning that unfortunate soul, Gunness beheaded her, and dressed the body in her own clothes. In an attempt to fool investigators, Belle removed her dental bridge, and placed it next to the victim.

On November 26, 1908 the jury acquitted Ray Lamphere of murder, but convicted him of arson. Judge J. C. Richter sentenced him to twenty years. On December 30, 1909 Lamphere died of tuberculosis in Michigan City Prison, but not before making a deathbed confession to Rev. E. A. Schell. Ray admitted to burying bodies for Belle, but solemnly swore that he never killed anyone. Her modus operandi was to fawn over new male invitees, cook them big meals, then drug their drinks. After guests passed out, she crushed their skulls with an ax, stole cash, jewelry, and clothing, then disposed of their remains on the farm.

Most La Porte residents believed that Belle survived the fire of April, 27, 1908. Neighbor Daniel Hutson sighted her on July 9, 1908.

> "I was coming from town with a hayrack, and saw Mrs. Gunness and a man walking in the orchard. Even at that distance I could recognize her ... I knew her shape, ... and lumbering walk. I never saw another woman who walked like her. She had on a light skirt, black (blouse,) wide-rimmed hat with black veil ... down to the chin and white veil over that. There was a man with her..."

Daniel Hutson's daughters Eldora and Evaline corroborated his story, as did two boys who were playing near Pine Lake Cemetery. Hutson added that Belle and her companion rushed to their buggy upon being spotted and raced away. He followed for a while, then thought the better of it, since "there was a good chance of me gettin' a chunk of lead."

In following years there were supposed sightings of Belle in Chicago, San Francisco, Los Angeles, Mississippi, and New York City. One unconfirmed rumor had her returning to Norway, another running a bordello in New Orleans. To this day no one knows Belle's ultimate fate.

THANK YOU FOR YOUR SERVICE[*]

—a review—

Eric Greinke

The collected poems of W. D. Ehrhart are a testimony to the principle that content eclipses style, a triumph of substance over surface. Ehrhart uses his relatively narrow palette to his advantage, to the effect that it is more accessible than poetry that is primarily decorous or lyrical. His colloquial language speaks to and for the common man, his target audience. Instead of trying to impress us with how clever or verbally gifted he is, Ehrhart's poetry focuses on human nature, especially in the context of conflicts ranging from big ones like war to interpersonal conflicts between individuals. He also explores inner-personal conflicts in several poems. On level one, his poems are cathartic. On a deeper level, they are redemptive. Ehrhart writes against the evil he perceives in himself and in humankind. His work departs significantly from that of previous generations of war poets, because it expresses doubt, guilt and criticism of the roles of soldiers and governments.

All of his poems are autobiographical and written in the first person, including a few translations from Vietnamese. Many of the poems examine the nature of hypocrisy, and Ehrhart never lets himself off the hook. Ehrhart is firmly in the confessional tradition, but avoids the narcissism of most confessionalists because of his courageous self-criticism, which is matched only by his indictment of society. Highly stylistic poetry is often a cover-up for a lack of serious content. If anything, Ehrhart errs in the opposite direction. He relies heavily on direct, often ironic statements and his subjects are seldom lighthearted. As a result, this is not an entertaining book, but it is a morally necessary one.

Over ninety percent of Ehrhart's poems refer to the Vietnam War and his experiences as a soldier, and are deeply anti-war. He is an ex-Marine who faced his shadow in the mirror. He saw the dark side of human nature and felt a moral responsibility to oppose it and clarify it for others. In his early poem "A Relative Thing," Ehrhart uses a collective persona to speak for soldiers everywhere: "We are the ones who have to live / with the memory that we were the instruments / of your pigeon-breasted fantasies / we are inextricable accomplices / in this travesty of dreams: / but we are not alone."

---

[*] *Thank You For Your Service: Collected Poems.* By W. D. Ehrhart. McFarland & Co., Inc., 2019. 278 pages. ISBN: 978-1-4766-7853-5.

Another fine early poem, "Rehoboth," also uses the third person persona effectively to speak on a universal level: "We have each other's love. / Friendship, though apart, shall still be common / to us all."

His poetry is at its best when his emotions are intense, and each poem has a realization at its core. Hope has wrestled with regret and anger throughout his writing career.

The Simple Lives of Cats

Cold spring rain drums hollow rhythms
on the windowpanes. Two a.m. The house
so dark and empty even the kittens
lie mesmerized by the echoing patter,
heads raised, ears twitching, eyes wide,
tiny noses sniffing the air for danger.

But the only danger here is me.
Once again I've lost it, temper flaring,
patience at a too-quick end, my daughter
crying, and my wife's heart sinking
in the sadness of another good day gone bad.
If sorry has a name, it must be mine.

The kittens don't suspect a thing.
One turns her head to lick my hand.
The other, having satisfied herself
this new sound filling up the night
is just another harmless curiosity,
stirs once, then settles in my lap.

Tonight my wife and child are sleeping
somewhere else. I've done this to myself
often enough to wonder just how many
chances I've got left. I stroke the cats,
who purr like engines; happy to be near,
they see no need for my improvement.

Ehrhart and I were both born in 1948, at the height of the post-WWII baby boom. We both enlisted in the military right out of high school, I in the Coast Guard, to save lives, and he in the Marines, to take them. While I'm sure that our experiences were radically different, I remember well the horror of those times and the pressure they put on young men near high school graduation. I lost two close friends from the graduating class ahead of mine within a few months of their arrival to fight in Vietnam. Another close friend came back a killer for America like Ehrhart. Short-sighted critics may call Ehrart a "one trick pony," but what he has done with his poetry is no mere trick. It is a deep commitment to the truth, and it took enormous courage to produce.

The image on the cover of this book is a photograph of W. D. Ehrhart as a young soldier in Vietnam, on a field of military green, a seemingly ironic persona for a poet, but Ehrhart is still a soldier. His battle is against the greed, ethnocentrism and brutality of human conflict.

Where did this long-term focus come from? Much of it must have come from his parents. His mother was a teacher and his father was a preacher. Although Ehrhart is a rebel, he is also deeply moral. His most personal poems deal with survivor's guilt and the long-term effects of post traumatic stress disorder. He has had a long-term problem with his own anger. His poem "The Damage We Do" examines the history of his anger and its effects on generations:

The Damage We Do

I don't know why I fell asleep
when I was eight at the top of the stairs
listening to my parents argue. Maybe I
thought they'd find me asleep and feel
so bad they'd learn how to get along.

I don't know why I put my fist
through the kitchen storm door glass
storming out of the house when I was ten,
but my mother had to wrap my hand
in a towel and call the doctor.
An accident, she said.

I don't know why I ran from the house
in my bare feet in February,
my father swearing, me in tears
and no clear thought but getting as far
away as a thirteen-year-old could get,

which wasn't far in a small town
where your dad's a minister, everyone
thinks he's a saint, and you're a disgrace
to be acting up the way you always do.

I don't remember a time when the house
I grew up in wasn't crackling with rage.
I don't know why. I think my father
was really a mess, but he didn't
discuss that with me, and my mother
just put up with him year after year.
You get so wired, you learn to think
that's the way life's supposed to be.

And you learn to be angry all the time.
You run away to California.
You join the Marines at seventeen.
You quit every job you don't get fired from.
After awhile you don't get hired,
and people avoid you; they think you're
out of control, and you probably are,
but it takes you most of a lifetime just
to begin to make the connections.

By then you've got a child of your own
who's angry all the time. I'd like to say
I don't know why, but I do.
I'd like to explain that it's not her fault,
but what's she supposed to do with that?
I'd like to undo the damage I've done,
but I don't know how.

This is as fine a confessional poem as I've read. We may conclude that he got both his anger and his moral concern in large part from his parents, however problematic that relationship may have been. The tension between conscience and anger became the aesthetic tension in his poems.

Ehrhart's form of confessionalism is justified by its universal relevancy to common human experience. He is no navel-gazer. Ultimately, his poems address the internal wars waged within each human heart. He understands the fundamental truth that a poem's moral message is its greatest value. For this great service, we really should be grateful.

THE MINISTRY OF TRUTH*

—a review—

John Rossi

Books about George Orwell appear with amazing regularity despite the fact he will be dead for seventy years in January 2020. No writer of the World War II generation or of the twentieth century for that matter has generated such interest among his followers and admirers. Since 1980 when his papers were opened, there have been at least five major biographies including the first by Bernard Crick to have full access to his private papers. Other major biographies have been published over the years by D.J. Taylor, Gordon Bowker, Michael Shelden and Jeffrey Meyers. All were outstanding in different ways.

In recent years studies of various aspects of Orwell's life also have appeared. To mention just a few: Robert Coles on Orwell as an English Rebel; Michael Brennan on Orwell's eccentric views of religion and most unusual of all, Thomas Ricks' Churchill and Orwell, a kind of dual biography. John Rodden, the first American to analyze Orwell's work in depth (*The Politics of Literary Reputation*) has edited a superb collection of essays, *The Cambridge Companion to George Orwell*, dealing with various themes of Orwell's life and times. As if that were not enough, Peter Davison, the dean of Orwell scholars, has compiled a 20 volume collection of all of Orwell's writings.

Every once in a while a book appears that perfectly captures the mood of the times. Why this is so is difficult to decipher. Partly it could as simple as saying well what people are thinking at a particular time. This apparently is the case Dorian Lynskey's new study of Orwell's dystopian novel, *1984*. Orwell's popularity and influence surfaces at times of political confusion such as ours. Thus the excitement over yet another examination of Orwell's most important and influential work.

All this leads to the question. Do we need another Orwell study? Since 2019 is the seventieth anniversary of the publication of *1984* we are getting them. The most heralded of the various recent writings about *1984* has been Dorian Lynskey's attempt to prepare a new biography of Orwell around his composition of *1984*. Lynskey's book has received nothing but praise both in

---

* Dorian Lynskey, *The Ministry of Truth: The Biography of George Orwell's 1984*. Doubleday, New York, 2019, $28.95.

England where it initially was published and equally positive reviews have appeared in all the key sites in the United States: *The New York Times*, *The Washington Post*, *Atlantic*, etc.

Among other things what makes Lynskey's book different is that he brings an unusual background to Orwell studies. His major interest has been in music and film and his most important publication is a study of protest songs. Orwell didn't have much to say about music in his writings and he spent a short time writing film reviews, hating the job all the time. So what does Lynskey have to say about Orwell and *1984* that is worth reading? In effect nothing particularly original, certainly little that you would not have garnered by reading any of the standard biographies. Yet Lynskey is still worth a read.

Lynskey argues that what justifies examining *1984* again is that it is the book we turn to when "truth is mutilated, language is distorted, power abused." (In case anyone misses the contemporary link, he mentions President Trump as the one he has in mind with those words. The seven pages critical of Trump in what is an Orwell biography may explain the book's popularity in English and American political circles.) But those were the very themes that readers highlighted when *1984* first appeared in June 1949 just as the Cold War settled in to the minds of people in the West. The Soviets would explode their atom bomb later that summer and the China fell to Mao's communist forces that fall. Since that summer *1984* has never been out of print and has appeared on the best seller list four times. In 1954 after the first television version was performed in England; in the eponymous year itself; in 2003, the centenary of Orwell's birth and most recently, after President Trump's election when one of his aids spoke about the existence of "alternate facts."

To enter Orwell's mind as he formulated the major themes of *1984*, Lynskey concentrates on what he regards were the formative forces in his thinking about utopias and dystopias. He begins with a long digression on the influence that the writer and prophet, H. G. Wells, had on Orwell. Orwell admitted that Wells was among major writers who shaped his thinking including his books about the future. "There you were in a world of pedants, clergymen and golfers," he wrote about his discovery of Wells, "and here was this wonderful man who could tell you about the inhabitants of the planets and the bottom of the sea, and who knew that the future was not going to be what respectable people imagined."

So Lynskey is on solid ground in studying Wells' influence on the young Orwell. But was it necessary to write a mini-biography of Wells and all his works where Orwell all but disappears in order to get show his influence on Orwell's thinking about the future? Similarly, Lynskey has a long section on Edward Bellamy and his book *Looking Backward*, stressing its influence all future utopian writing. All very interesting, but to what purpose? I checked four of the major biographies of Orwell and Bellamy is not cited once. In the four volumes of Orwell's *Collected Essays, Journalism and Letters*, one of the foundation sources for Orwell studies, there isn't a single reference to Bellamy.

Long digressions like this pop up throughout the book. The most annoying are related to what must be central too much of Lynskey's thinking—the role of music in shaping culture. When he drifts into this realm not only does Orwell disappear but the writing takes on the vagueness of much popular culture prose. Eight pages on David Bowie's cultural significance may be interesting to music fans but the link to Orwell is weak. Even worse are examples of what I call fashionable pop culture writing. An interesting discussion of how Ayn Rand's work fits into utopian thinking leads to Lynskey's thoughts on George Lucas' film *THYX1138*, the Canadian band, Rush, and Ben Elton and Queen's hit 2002 musical, *We Will Rock You*. Even worse, this kind of digression is followed by what he must regard as a profound observation. "The winding path from Lenin to Lego (the movie) illustrates that anti-utopian narratives have the flexibility and portability of myths." There is entirely too much of this intellectual jargon throughout the book.

Lynskey is on firmer ground when he analyzes the more concrete forces that shaped Orwell's thinking. He doesn't devote much attention to Orwell's youth, his schooling, his service in Burma or his attempt to identify with those living on the margin of society in London and Paris. These experiences generated important writings for Orwell including one of his better novels, *Burmese Days* and his popular investigation of life on the edge, *Down and Out in Paris and London*. Lynskey believes that elements of *1984* leaked into Orwell's brilliant and brutal indictment of his school days, "Such, Such Were the Joys," which was written around the time he was working on his dystopian masterpiece.

Orwell's early writings until *Road to Wigan Pier*, his investigation of poverty and unemployment among the poor of Northern England written in 1937, are also quickly passed over. Orwell's novels other than *Coming Up For Air* which Lynskey sees as presaging much of the grim world of *1984* are dismissed as "junk shops piled to the rafters with miscellaneous preoccupations for which he couldn't find a more suitable home."

Lynskey believes that the unique Orwell style, what he often refers to as his voice, really only matured after the Spanish Civil War, the event that largely reshaped his political thinking. I believe he overstresses the point about Orwell developing his style only after his Spanish experiences. Before he went to Spain in 1936 he had already demonstrated a high degree of literary sophistication in his essays, "A Hanging" and "Shooting an Elephant" which make a powerful case against the death penalty and the corrupting effect of imperialism on the ruler as well as the ruled.

Lynskey is on firmer grounds in his analysis of the Spanish Civil War on Orwell's thoughts about totalitarianism thought. The line from Spain to *Animal Farm* and *1984* is a direct one. Spain showed Orwell as Lynskey notes the "nightmare world that pervades *1984*, what Orwell called the poisonous broth of rumors, lies, smears and paranoia led you "to feel like a conspirator" even if you were innocent

Orwell went to Spain to fight fascism but came away hating communism. He would criticize it energetically because he believed communism was a more treacherous ideology that covered its evil side by nobler aims. Spain also taught him how the reporting on the war, especially by left wing newspaper and journals, was based on lies and distortions of the truth. In his essay "Looking Back on the Spanish War," published in 1943, he wrote that he saw "history being written not terms of what happened but of what ought to have happened according to various party lines." He feared for the first time that the very concept of objective truth was disappearing in the modern world, a major theme that would be central to *1984*.

Lynskey ranks Orwell's memoir of his time in Spain, *Homage to Catalonia* as important in the development of his ideas about totalitarianism even though the book only sold 750 copies during his lifetime. It has since become one of the classic studies of the complexities of the Spanish Civil War.

When World War II broke out, Orwell tried to find a place for his talents. His poor health kept him from the military. He had already suffered bouts of the lung problems that foreshadowed the tuberculosis that would eventually kill him in 1950. He eventually joined the BBC, spending two years as a broadcaster of Allied propaganda to India. Unlike many Orwell scholars, Lynskey believes that these were not wasted years. His time at the BBC provided Orwell with the corporate environment that he could expand upon for Winston Smith's time at the Ministry of Truth in *1984*. Lynskey also believes that those months gave Orwell a chance to think and mature the ideas that he would later flesh out in *Animal Farm* and *1984*: "ruminations on war, politics, totalitarianism and literature that would prepare the ground for his two great works of fiction and his finest essays."

The last part of Lynskey's book focuses on the writing of *1984* itself. For *1984*, Orwell was deeply influenced by his reading of various utopian and dystopian novels. In particular he was impressed by the novel *We* written by a refugee from the Russian Revolution, Yevgeny Zamyatin. *We* crystalized many of the ideas that Orwell had reflected on about a future totalitarian state. Along with *We*, Lynskey believes that the two works that most influenced Orwell in shaping his view of future gone wrong were Wells' *The Sleeper Awakes* and Aldous Huxley's *Brave New World*, rival prophecies of what the future holds. *Brave New World* in particular provided Orwell a vision of a "glittering sinister world in which society has hardened into a caste system and the workers are permanently enslaved."

Lynskey is carefully dismissive of the controversy that Orwell borrowed heavily from the dystopian novel *Swastika Night* written by a woman author, Katherine Burdekin, under the pseudonym Murray Constantine. The feminist critic Daphne Patai built an entire book around the argument that Orwell stole many of the themes in *1984* from Burdekin's book. There were definite similarities in the two approaches to a totalitarian future and it was published in 1937 by the Left Book Club which Orwell was familiar with having written *The Road to Wigan Pier* for them that year. There is no evidence, however, the Orwell read the book or discussed it with any of his friends.

One thing Lynskey sets out to do is demolish the idea that *1984* was the work of a morbid, dying man. Lynskey believes that whatever flaws there are in *1984* as to character development or plot cannot be attributed to Orwell's poor health. As he was writing *1984* Orwell had many other projects in mind, a list of which can be found in a notebook he kept, including a short story for which he already had a title, "A Smoking Room Story," as well as long essay on the novelist Evelyn Waugh. Having proposed to a handful of women after the death of his first wife, shortly before his death he married for the second time a beautiful young woman, Sonia Brownell. Hardly the action of someone with a death wish.

Lynskey's book is an untraditional biography of Orwell in many ways under the guise of tracing the evolution of *1984*. It is generally well written and interspersed with different ways of looking at Orwell and his career. If there is a criticism it would be the existence of too many digressions into areas that might interest Lynskey but really had little to do with Orwell or even *1984* for that matter. Still it is an interesting addition to the many studies that Orwell's writings have inspired and will probably continue to inspire.

STORISENDE

Karen Greenbaum-Maya

Some stories go to the end of their world, Narnia and Fillory, Middle Earth and Earthsea. Their end is always the longest journey, far past pleasure. Pleasure doesn't matter anymore. Waters at the end are uncharted. You see the mountain far away, far beyond your little strength. Your wooden boat leaks. Magic drives it streaking over open seas where no rain falls, so far west that you leave behind the stars you knew. There is no guide but your memories of failures, the beggar you refused, the friend you betrayed for flimsy praise from a stranger. The food you could carry is gone. New stars are brighter than the world you knew. Not hard when that world has gone so dull.

The end is empty of everything except its ending. It is the opposite of lovely. Fog, or sunlight bleaching bones. Your eyes sting, you retch against caustic air. No Galapagos finches, no evolution to flourish in the passage of time. No blue flower of a new plant sprouting from the hero's heart. Perhaps, dragons. Or border agents, to stamp your papers one last time. Authors seem pleased with their agents, capricious and officious. Bureaucracy keeps the edges tight. No sailing away into the air, leaving that earth in triumph as the locals watch you turn into a pinpoint.

These worlds are flat like buttons, like coins. Mountains make the rim. You climb up over the peak, moving along the flip of up into down, first heavy then adrift. What can it feel like, to slam against your empty self before you find your way? All agree: reaching the end of the world changes you. No one will really believe you.

The long way around is the short way home. So say all the books. Their heroes return in a blink. By now, everyone is tired out. What a let-down, to finish the book, to go back to your life.

ON GUARD

Karen Greenbaum-Maya

Can we ever be clever enough, even we who are the best of them all? We see how the wind is blowing. It blows from the outside. There can never be enough protection from impurities, from the eager dangers that skulk everywhere, working day and night to get at you, dangers like gangs of children, children of migrants just arrived from the South who always expect good folk—like us!—to take care of them, dangers like nervous small dogs that could bite, like the sneaky farmers, former salt of the earth, who feed their livestock grain and grass sprayed with poisons. They say it's organic, but you cannot be too careful. There is no enduring harbor from the malice of the world. Okay, maybe for an hour or a day, but not for good, never for long. Not even we are clever enough for that.

Organized gangs of children will snatch at the thin gold chain that entwines with your hollow golden heart. They'll snatch at your old iPhone. If you have it they want it and they will take it from you. How can you still be too calm? You must be harder, angrier, more alarmed. Your eyes must draw the fear from your legs and push it back into their eyes, compel them to give way before you.

SACRED

Karen Greenbaum-Maya

Wolf is just one way to get there. Vievee Francis, "All Kinds of Howlin'"

How can you know your totem, your spirit animal? She says Beyoncé is her spirit animal, he says his totem is a lion. But it's just conversation, almost a joke. What if Beyoncé doesn't consent to be anyone's spirit anything, what if his lion is a cat? How can you know for sure? Is it like being born Jewish, like being born into a church? or like the Cub Scouts, growling with the Grizzlies, howling with the Wolfpack? and why never Squirrel or Gray Rat, not even Jackrabbit?

Clearly they are true cubs. They know they will grow into the clan of their godbeast. It is written. They know the signs, the rightness of their paws and claws, the knots they worry from their fur, all the marks of the big warm animals they see around them. At best I was a deformed duckling, my bones too big for my skin, knees that didn't know which way to fold, all my clumsy moves revealing mid-flinch a gritty gray duckling and nothing more, nothing else, working out the world from scratch, no grown bird nearby to point the way.

But when at last I heard what the poet wrote about Howling Wolf, how he'd been her lover preacher teacher, I told her *Howling Wolf is your spirit animal*. She laughed and said I was a seer. Said for sure I had a calling.

IDENTITY POLITICS

Peter Tonery

Cliff went alone to the Wheeling Community Center to hear the newest, "rising-star" poet. He was Cliff's age, but Asian American and gay. Cliff learned to love poetry serving in Iraq; starting with Hip-Hop, evolved to Atwood, then Li Young Lee. This young poet disappointed. His poems were fruity glacés; tight, controlled narratives about coming out and pining for the love of school boys he'd never have. This is not pain! Cliff thought; then, despite his desperate panicky efforts, he watched again as his best friend took a bullet through the teeth in that blazing desert. No kissing here either.

THE SLOT

Raymond Deej

I hurriedly tipped and closed my glasses and book when she came to me, spilling into the chair, carrying both drinks, half empty now, gone down her arms and onto her dress.

"I've been watching you," she said.

"I know," I said.

"My husband has gone off crying over his bad luck and my terrible listening."

Indeed, I had seen the husband trudge off our little restaurant patio. This following what appeared a slanted discussion over the recent death of a transient daughter. For him, it was difficult to draw a line between sadness and regret, where one left off and the other began. He hoped she agreed. And if they could manage at least the line, *THE LINE*, then they could craft a list of all things which were theirs, the daughter's, or nobody's fault, and in this way formalize their grief and—

Now the husband reappeared. He seemed not to notice the seating change, and casually took his place beside her. He drank and looked off, grimacing. She rubbed his arm and kissed it.

"Relax, you crazy," she said.

Then he turned to me, poised.

"Our names are Posh, Joseph and Christine," he said. "We own a house and a lion. Last month he ripped our friend Sanjeev's arm off. We feed Animaniac buckets of crack corn and donuts twice daily through the slot. Sanjeev misjudged his reach. Truly, it must have felt like God. The sudden force. The impact. And though we are sorry, in many ways we couldn't live without its happening. Nor could Sanjeev." Joseph looked to Christine with a pensive gaze, and Christine tilted her head and smiled softly, as if to say that while the plight of Sanjeev was hurtful, it was true, and because it was true it was good. Then she said:

"Joseph has cancer and we've been struggling, you know."

Joseph winced with annoyance, holding up a hand.

"What we wonder," he said, "is if you would leave with us this evening, and feed Animaniac his donuts and corn."

His look was tender, Christine's expectant. The air was brisk and the evening sky a furious orange. I suspect my eyes glistened just then, and with a sudden randomness I ought credit to a radiant, disorienting woman I once crippled in self-defense, to loneliness, and to the childhood death of my mother by my father's bathtub poison soap, I said yes. Immediately.

* * *

We parked atop a stone driveway. En route, Christine slept and I became sick, yet by Joseph imparting best practices for car-window vomiting I'd arrived feeling both revived and clean. Leaving Christine we entered the home through double-doors of white walnut and stylishly corroded hardware, and encountered an enormous yet crude painting of a cactus and a bear, titled "Cactus y Bear." I stared at it; then followed Joseph down a concrete-walled passageway until he stopped and set his ear to a door.

"Sanjeev's room," he said. "He's been on voice protest for science. Less talk, more science evidently. Before the lion he could not have approached this. We are proud, and will tell him when he shows."

We walked on, and soon before us opened a ballroom and the great cage, which seemed a fortress within a home. Five paces in sat the lion, a shockingly lean, even gaunt creature, upright and turned away.

Here Joseph set a bucket at my feet, disappeared, and then returned carrying Christine in both arms, slapping at her face. She roused and the two took their place at the rear, Joseph tall, alert, Christine weary, smiling. They held hands, and Joseph said:

"Be mindful. Connect with him. See him first as you would a person, in spite of what you imagine he'll do."

"Alright," I said.

"And once fed so too will we feast, over bread, pork, wine, and say about all we've loved and lost—confess to our best and worst transactions."

"Alright," I said, and moved forward to the cage.

Upon reaching the slot—that flimsy, retractable door for feeding—the lion turned to face, and I softened my eyes to show how I knew him well, adhering to Joseph's instruction. Yet for me the lion could not reciprocate, and what he communicated instead, unambiguously and to my horror, was pain. Not a wincing pain, nor a burning one, but a foreboding anguish come of this discourteous moment and its contributing factors: The drunken, gluttonous circumstance surrounding his captivity, its duration, the fiscal reasoning behind donuts and corn and his starvation, so then the plight of Sanjeev, who he secretly loved, and the plight now of me, who he was capable of loving, and yet—

At the lion's anguish, I dropped to a knee and began to weep. It was a difficult time. Yet soon a hand rested on my shoulder.

"You must discover what will happen," Christine said lovingly. "We've seen you around. Alone. For so long. Pretending to read that enormous book."

SARAH

Javanse' Ryland-Buntley

She could hear his footsteps walking down the stairs, slowly. The smell of alcohol fills the room. He must have had a bad day. He had been having a lot of those recently. That just meant he would show extra love tonight. That was the routine: bad day, drink, extra love.

"Sarah!" he sang. His voice caressing each syllable, soft and cunning

She stepped off the chair that was facing the window. There wasn't much to see, except for the dead gardenias, overgrown weeds, and the occasional insect. Yesterday, it was the angry bee; today, a grasshopper. She never stared out the window for the view per se, rather a glimpse of the outside. *What season was it? Was it really as warm and sunny as it looked?*

She lifted the chair, her frail body using all of its muscle. She had to be very quiet, or he'll hear. She set the chair on the other side of the room upside down. Her arms shaking, inches away from giving up. *Don't.* She looked up toward the stairs. His tall lanky body, nothing but a mere shadow to her. She shivered at the thought of one day seeing him up close again, she had been deprived for months. He hadn't made it all the way down yet. *Good.* She still had time. Her fingers let go of the chair after they were certain it was securely on the ground; then, they moved swiftly to the shirt. She began unbuttoning his blue dress shirt, setting it over the chair. Making sure it was just as he left it. She knew he wouldn't remember, but she did it, just in case.

"Sarah." His voice wasn't slurred and incomprehensible, like it usually was when he drank. *Shit.* She hadn't prepared for this. She quickly dropped, her bony knees hitting the ground with a faint thud. She looked back at the stairs, he hadn't noticed. She crawled back to the window and sat against the wall. Reaching towards the broken heater adjacent to her, she slid her hand back through the handcuff. She tapped the ground around her. *Where is it?* Her hand shaking as she felt for the strip of cloth he made her wear. She didn't understand. *Why blind her from him?* His beautiful face was already tattooed in her brain. *There it is.*

"Sarah, you're going to be really proud of me." She could hear the satisfaction in his voice. "I didn't drink one sip today. I know I smell like it, but someone threw some at me." He paused, "So, maybe, I had a trickle of it." She could just imagine the smile on his face as he spoke. Her face lit up thinking about that confident voice she had fallen in love with that very first day of fifth grade.

She remembered sitting in the back corner of the classroom. She was staring at birds, two cardinals, playing a game of Hide n' Seek. He walked in the room, his brown hair slicked back, his blue dress shirt tucked into a pair of khakis. His voice, assertive and smooth. He claimed all the students' attention with a simple, "Good morning." She even thought the birds had stopped what they were doing to pay attention. The power in that voice captivated her. It made her stay after class every day to hear more about each species of animal and their mating rituals. She remembered him whispering to her before recess as he slipped her the gift of his number; "You're my favorite," he said. She had wanted to tell him the same, but the words never came out. Her smile said it all.

"Your parents were on the news this morning."

The hairs on the back of her neck stood up. *Parents. When did she last see them?* She could recall seeing their faces that morning. They took a picture, commemorating the last day of fifth grade. She had told them she was going to Amy's after school. That was a lie. He told her she couldn't tell them that he was taking her to the zoo. "Our secret," he said. *Our secret.* She put on her biggest smile for the photo, while they kissed both of her cheeks. *Did she remember to tell them she loved them?*

A loud creak sounded from the stairs. He had reached the bottom. Her hands uncontrollably shaking as she fumbled with the cloth, trying to pull it over her lion's mane of messy curls. *Too late.*

"So, you want to be a bad girl?" She looked past him at the blue fabric that once covered her modesty. "Huh!" he screamed, his breath wrapping around her neck. She could feel his moist hands on her body, pushing her head into the cold concrete ground. He got behind her, the handcuffs rattling against the heater. The clatter of his belt buckle. She wanted to scream, but this was his way of showing his love. She held her breath, praying he will have a good day tomorrow. "They've all given up on you." His voice, an uncontrolled fire in her ears, "they think you're dead." Her face grew hot. *Why wouldn't he tell them she was fine? Didn't he love her?* Her body rocked back and forth, his grunts filled the quiet room. *Who was this monster?* It just couldn't—it couldn't be—Mr. Fitzgerald, her favorite teacher, the only man she ever loved.

ABANDONMENT

Pat Hanahoe-Dosch

In January the blue in the sky disappears in our part of New Jersey. Even on the rare occasion when it isn't cloudy, our world is filled with just sand, a few bare trees, and a lot of empty houses waiting for the summer/ weekend people to come back. In fall and winter I nickname this place The Abandonment. After Memorial Day, tourists and summer residents return, and the whole island is rescued from ruin again.

In this small bagel shop it's warm and—pardon the pun—toasty. Every morning I open the shop at 5:00 a.m. By then, the baker has already filled most of the bins. Customers love the smell of this place, but to be honest, I don't even notice the smells anymore. My favorite is whole wheat with plain cream cheese. That's usually breakfast because I can eat for free here. I'm saving up to go away to the state university in a couple of years. Maybe. I'm taking a math class at the community college two nights a week, now. Mom gave me the tuition money as my graduation gift. She says I have to keep going to school because if I stop, I might not ever go back. "Look at me," she usually says when I grumble about homework. "I got married right after high school and never went back. I thought I knew everything. Look at me now—a single mom waiting tables six days a week and can't even get ahead with all that overtime." I'm not sure if she regrets having me more than not going to college, but I hear her message. She says it often enough. I'm working hard at this class, harder than I did in high school where, to be honest, I didn't do much. Why work hard when you know you can't afford to go anywhere anyway?

The shop is owned by a man who lives in Philly most of the time but has a gorgeous big house two blocks from here, facing the ocean, which he visits on weekends in the summer. I live four blocks away from the beach in a small, old house my mom inherited from her mom. We're still cleaning mold out of the laundry room from Hurricane Sandy. The manager of the bagel shop, Miriam, also runs the deli across the street, so she lets me and Frankie basically run everything. I open, and Frankie closes. If we have a problem, we can run across the street and ask for help or an answer, but we don't get many problems here selling bagels. I mean, who'd have a problem with bagels?

We're only open until 3:00 p.m., anyway. Our rush time is from 6:00 a.m. till about 10:00 a.m. on weekends and the summer. The rest of the time, we just get a few locals and stragglers. And Louie.

Louie hangs out by the corner most of the night. He pretends he's waiting for a bus, but his particular bus never comes. It's always the next one. I think he sleeps on the bench under the bus stop sign. He sits up when he hears me unlocking the door in the mornings. "Hey Kimmie," he always says. "Got any leftover bagels from yesterday?"

I always save him one. We give the rest to the homeless shelter on the other end of the island though in the summer there isn't usually much left over. In winter, there're too many leftovers, but Miriam says to keep baking and selling what we can—I nicknamed her Always Hopeful, but never call her that out loud. The other side of the island is where most of the poor are. On our end, in summer we're over run by the rich who own second homes here, but this time of year, it's mostly just us locals. Some of us may be just hanging on, but we're not soup kitchen poor. We make a living off the rich and the tourists here one way or another.

Then there's Louie. I guess there are others like him, but I don't see them. Once in a while there'll be another guy hanging out at the bus stop with him, but they never stick around. Louie, though, he seems to like drinking at the Sailfish bar until it closes. He always smells of stale beer and sweat, mixed with a faint whiff of urine. He's sad, and I understand sad. I always figured someone abandoned him, too. I nicknamed him The Abandoned Bum, but I don't call him that. I let him into the shop with me and toast whatever kind of leftover bagel I set aside in a bag under the cash register the day before. He likes cream cheese with chives, so that's what I smear on it. Sometimes he has enough to buy a coffee, but sometimes he doesn't. He looks real bad today, so I figure he probably doesn't.

"Don't tell anyone," I say, as usual.

"Thank you," he says, taking the bagel in both hands and lifting it to his nose to smell it. "Mmm."

"Here," I say, handing him a cup of coffee. "The coffee's on me today. You look like you need it. What'd you do to yourself last night?"

"God bless you, girl," he says. "I may have had a bit to drink last night. I was celebrating. Yesterday was the feast of Queen Esther, you know."

"Hunh," I grunt, wiping down the counter. "You mean Purim. I'm Jewish, too. I know it was Purim yesterday." Actually, I hadn't known that. We aren't religious. But I knew all about Queen Esther. When I was little, my mom did tell me the stories behind all the holidays.

I think I know what's coming. This is the real reason I feed Louie and let him hang out at the shop for an hour or so in the mornings. Louie tells stories—not always well, but they are always funny in some way or another. He entertains not just me, but the customers, too. Already there's a line of three people, all regulars who stop here to grab breakfast on their way to work. I take their orders and start gathering bagels, filling a bag with a dozen for one, making bagel and egg sandwiches for another, pouring coffee for the third who can't decide if he wants a poppy or onion bagel. I think he just wants to hear Louie's story. We know it will not be the traditional Bible story.

"She was my ancestor," he says. I laugh. He looks at me with a sad squint. I refill the coffee pot and try to look serious. It's more likely that I'll graduate from Harvard Law School than that Louie is descended directly from Queen Esther of the Bible.

"The way most people tell that story," he says, "it's all about Mordecai. But really, the hero of the story is Queen Esther. She's the one who saved our people. She was a strong woman, like my own Esther, God rest her soul." He stops and looks down at his coffee. He hasn't taken the plastic lid off of the Styrofoam cup yet. "And that's because the queen's father died before she was born, and her mother died giving birth to her, so she was always alone, orphaned, even in the house of her uncle. Of course, she wasn't queen then, just a scared Jewish girl." He pauses for a minute. He looks out the big display window at the front of the shop. "Like my Esther," he says. "She was always scared because she was an orphan, too. Her aunt and uncle raised her with their kids, but she never belonged, she told me. She never belonged any-where until she married me. But then she died," he says. "I was driving, and we crashed. And now she's with Queen Esther somewhere."

He's silent for a moment. Then he says, "But Esther, she knew how to get what she wanted. In the end, the king gave her everything and all the Jews rose up and killed all their enemies. It was a great victory, but a sad time for everyone else. Death is a terrible business," he says. He leans forward, over the counter to me and says quietly, "I think she wants revenge on me, too. She comes looking for me sometimes at night and tries to stab me with the cold. But I keep waking up." He walks out the door, slowly, with his coffee in one hand and the paper wrapped bagel in the other.

The customer who was listening turns to me. "Onion," he says. I toast his bagel, butter it, and give it to him. He pays me. "Not the usual kind of story from Louie," he says. "Man, I feel bad for the guy."

"Yeah," I say, "Me too." He leaves. I watch Louie from the front win-dow. He sits on the bus bench, hunched over, eating his bagel just like he's done countless mornings before. His stained wool coat looks a little shabbier than usual. I want to go out there and hug him or something, maybe tell him about my dad who left us when I was little. Mom says sometimes that he can't handle responsibility, that's why he left, but sometimes I think it's because my twin died when we were infants. She just stopped breathing, mom says. I want to tell Louie I know about death, too, but I don't remember her, or my dad. I just know them from photos. Maybe he blames me because I didn't die too. I don't ask mom about that any more. She never answers my questions, just says some things are better left in the past. She works all the time because we don't have insurance or much else, except bills. We have lots of bills.

In high school, I thought not having a dad made me The Abandoned Kid. I tried to find him once, a couple years ago. There are lots of ways of finding someone on the Internet. It looks like he's been living in Las Vegas, going from one job to another, one apartment to another. A bum, my mom says. I picture him like Louie, sleeping at bus stops, hungry and lonely. In my head, that made me think I could bond with Louie somehow. Like we're kindred spirits or something, but today I realize we're not. In a weird way, it's kind of a relief, but still cruel. I pour another cup of coffee and take it out to him. "Here," I say, handing it to him as I sit on the bench. "You look like today's gonna be at least a two cup kind of day."

He squints up at me because the sun is coming up and the day is getting kind of bright. For once, it isn't cloudy. Spring must be close. He's always squinting, I think. He doesn't ever look straight at anybody, as far as I can tell. "Thanks," he says. "Queen Esther is gonna save us all, you know. She did it before. She will again."

"Hey," someone calls from the shop. "Are you open or what? I gotta get to work. I need to bring a dozen bagels with me for a meeting."

"Sure," I say, more to Louie than the customer. "Whatever." Frankie should be here soon to help out. I usually re-tell Louie's stories to him. Not today though. There isn't a story to tell. Not one he'd want to listen to, anyway.

I guess no one wants to listen to the real stories, the ones that aren't funny or made up out of wishes. I hope Louie will be funny again tomorrow. I count on him to be funny. I have to get back to work, then later go home, make dinner so my mom won't have to when she gets home, exhausted, and I won't ask my mom anything about my dad, again, though I want to, because I know she'll never tell me more than she has. My dad probably isn't anything like Louie. He probably isn't that guy on the Internet, but has a job and a house and another family, by now. I know he's never coming back. I have to make up my own stories. Maybe I should work on making them funny like Louie does, most of the time, but I don't know how to make something funny anymore than I know how to find someone who's missing. For all I know, that guy I found on the Internet could have been just someone who had the same name. But it's the only story I have of him. I want to believe someone gives him a bagel and coffee sometimes. Maybe someone listens to him sometimes. Maybe he tells stories about me.

R. A. Allen's poetry has appeared in *RHINO Poetry, The Penn Review, Gargoyle, Mantis, Night Train, Glassworks, JAMA, Rendez-Vous*, and elsewhere, His fiction has been published in *The Literary Review, The Barcelona Review, PANK, The Los Angeles Review*, and *Best American Mystery Stories 2010*, among others. He lives in Memphis and was born on the same day the Donner Party resorted to cannibalism: December 26th. More at https://poets.nyq.org/poet/raallen

Visual artist **Desirée Alvarez**'s first book, *Devil's Paintbrush*, won the 2015 May Sarton New Hampshire Poetry Prize. Anthologized in *What Nature and Other Musics: New Latina Poetry* and published in *Boston Review, Fence, Iowa Review* and *Poetry*, she has received the Glenna Luschei Poetry Award from Prairie Schooner and awards from NYFA, Poets House and the American Academy of Arts and Letters. She teaches at CUNY and the Juilliard School.

Chris Bullard lives in Philadelphia, PA. He received his B.A. in English from the University of Pennsylvania and his M.F.A. from Wilkes University. Finishing Line Press published his poetry chapbook, *Leviathan*, in 2016 and Kattywompus Press published *High Pulp*, a collection of his flash fiction, in 2017. His work has appeared in recent issues of *Nimrod, Muse/A Journal, The Woven Tale, Red Coyote, Cutthroat* and *The Offbeat*.

Joseph Cilluffo's first book of poetry, *Always in the Wrong Season*, was recently published by Kelsay Books and is available on amazon.com. His poems have also appeared in journals such as Philadelphia Poets, Apiary, and Philadelphia Stories. Joe was the Featured Poet for the Fall 2014 Edition of the Schuylkill Valley Journal, which nominated his poem, Light, for the Pushcart Prize.

Mike Cohen hosts Poetry Aloud and Alive at Philadelphia's Big Blue Marble Book Store. His articles on sculpture regularly appear in *Schuylkill Valley Journal*. His wry writing has appeared in the *Mad Poets Review, Apiary Magazine, Fox Chase Review*, and other journals. Mike's poetry can be found at www.mikecohensays.com and in his book *Between the I's*.

Joan Colby's *Selected Poems* received the 2013 FutureCycle Prize and *Ribcage* was awarded the 2015 Kithara Book Prize. Her recent books include *Her Heartsongs* published by Presa Press and *Joyriding to Midnight* from FutureCycle Press.

Barbara Daniels' *Rose Fever: Poems* was published by WordTech Press and her chapbooks *Moon Kitchen, Black Sails*, and *Quinn & Marie* by Casa de

Cinco Hermanas Press. She received three individual artist fellowships from the New Jersey State Council on the Arts and earned an MFA in poetry at Vermont College. Her poems have appeared in *Prairie Schooner, Mid-American Review, WomenArts Quarterly Journal, The Literary Review*, and many other journals.

Raymond Deej lives in Idaho with his kids. That's everything. The daughter's been making the rules.

Pat Hanahoe-Dosch's story, "Sighting Bia," was a finalist for A Room of Her Own Foundation's 2012 Orlando Prize. Her stories have been published in *The Peacock Journal, In Posse Review, Sisyphus*, and *Schuylkill Valley Journal*. Her poetry has been in many publications and two books. See her website http://pathanahoedosch.blogspot.com/

Tim Gavin is an Episcopal priest, serving as head chaplain at The Episcopal Academy. Prolific Press Released his chapbook, *Lyrics from the Central Plateau*, in November 2018. He is currently developing a manuscript: *Divine Property*. His poems have appeared in *The Anglican Theological Review, Blue Heron Review, Blue Mountain Review, Cape Rock, Cardinal Sins, Chiron Review, Digital Papercut, Evening Street Review, Magma, Poetry Quarterly* and *Spectrum*. He lives with his wife in Newtown Square, PA.

Ray Greenblatt teaches a Joy of Poetry course at Temple-OLLI University. He has been published in: *Comstock Review, Ibbetson Street, International Poetry Review, Midwest Quarterly* among others. His experimental novel *Twenty Years on Graysheep Bay* is half-poetry and half-Flash Fiction. His most recent book of poetry is *Nocturnes & Aubades* (Parnilis Press, 2018).

Karen Greenbaum-Maya, retired psychologist, German major, two-time Pushcart and Best of the Net nominee and occasional photographer, is keeping on. Her work appears in venues including *B O D Y, Sow's Ear Poetry Review, Comstock Poetry Review, Naugatuck Poetry Review*, and *Measure*. Kattywompus Press publishes her three chapbooks, *Burrowing Song, Eggs Satori*, and now *Kafka's Cat*. Kelsay Books publishes *The Book of Knots and their Untying*. She co-curates Fourth Sundays, a poetry series in Claremont, California. Links to her work at: www.cloudslikemountains.blogspot.com/.

Eric Greinke has new work in/and forthcoming: *The Bryant Literary Review, Coe Review, Ibbetson Street, Lake Effect, Loch Raven Review, North Dakota Quarterly, Over The Transom, Pennsylvania English, Poetry Pacific* (Canada),

Prairie Schooner, Taj Mahal Review (India), *Trajectory,* and *Rosebud.* His most recent books are: *Shorelines* (Adastra Press, 2018) and *Invisible Wings* (Presa Press, 2019). His book *For The Living Dead—New & Selected Poems* (Presa Press, Simon Pulse, 2014) was nominated for a Pulitzer Prize. He lives in an old stone cottage by a lake in Western Michigan. www.ericgreinke.com

Luray Gross is the author of four collections of poetry, most recently *Lift,* published by Ragged Sky Press of Princeton, NJ. A storyteller as well, Gross works extensively in New Jersey and Pennsylvania as an Artist in Residence. She was awarded a Fellowship in Poetry from the NJ Council on the Arts and has served as resident faculty for the Frost Place Conference on Poetry. She is one of Bucks County PA's poets laureate.

Don Hogle's poetry has appeared recently in *Apalachee Review, Atlanta Review, Carolina Quarterly, Chautauqua, The Inquisitive Eater* (The New School), *South Florida Poetry Journal,* and *A3 Review* and *Shooter* in the U.K. Among other awards, he won First Prize in the 2016 Hayden's Ferry Review poetry contest and received an Honorable Mention for the 2018 E. E. Cummings Prize from the New England Poetry Club. He lives in Manhattan. www.donhoglepoet.com

Phil Huffy had a professional career doing something else entirely. In middle age, he found his voice as a poet and has discovered much to speak about. He generally works on one piece at a time, often at his kitchen table in Western New York. Writing in a variety of styles, he has achieved placement in dozens of publications, including *The Lyric, Hedge Apple, Magnolia Review, Fourth & Sycamore* and *The Road Not Taken.*

A three-time Pushcart Prize nominee and Pennsylvania Bucks County Poet Laureate, **Marie Kane** has published three collections of lyric and narrative poems: *Survivors in the Garden* (Big Table Publishing, 2012), which mostly concerns her life with multiple sclerosis, *Beauty, You Drive a Hard Bargain* (Kelsay Press, 2017), and *Persephone's Truth* (2018), with art by her husband, Stephen Millner. Her poetry is published in *The Belleview Literary Review, Naugatuck River Review* and many others. See mariekanepoetry.com.

Vasiliki Katsarou's poems have been published in *NOON: Journal of the Short Poem* (Japan), *Reliquiae* (U.K.), *Regime Journal* (Australia), *otata,* as well as *Poetry Daily* and *Tiferet.* She is the author of the collection *Memento Tsunami,* and read her poetry in the 2014 Dodge Poetry Festival. Currently affiliated with New Jersey's Hunterdon Art Museum, Vasiliki has also written and directed an award-winning 35mm short film, *Fruitlands 1843*, about a Transcendentalist utopian community in Massachusetts.

Named one of the "100 Most Influential People in Brooklyn Culture" by Brooklyn Magazine, **Jason Koo** is the founder and executive director of Brooklyn Poets and creator of the Bridge. He is the author of the poetry collections *More Than Mere Light, America's Favorite Poem* and *Man on Extremely Small Island* and coeditor of the *Brooklyn Poets Anthology*. The winner of fellowships from the National Endowment for the Arts, Vermont Studio Center and New York State Writers Institute, he earned his BA in English from Yale, his MFA in creative writing from the University of Houston and his PhD in English and creative writing from the University of Missouri-Columbia. He is an associate teaching professor of English at Quinnipiac University and lives in Williamsburg.

Matt Lake is a sometime science journalist, erstwhile technologist, and frequent public speaker, with bylines in *The New York Times, San Francisco Chronicle, Entertainment Weekly,* and *Scientific American*. None of this counts for too much, however, as he is best known for his work editing and writing for the *Weird U.S.* book series.

Will Reger is the 2019-20 Inaugural Poet Laureate to the city of Urbana, IL, a founding member of the Champaign-Urbana Poetry Group (cupoetry. com). He has a Ph.D. from UIUC, teaches at Illinois State University in Normal, and has published in the *Blue Nib Literary Magazine, Passager Journal, Eclectica Magazine, Broadkill Review,* and the *Innesfree Poetry Journal*. His chapbook is *Cruel with Eagles*. He is at https://twitter.com/wmreger—or wandering in the woods playing his flute.

Edwin Romond's most recent book is *Home Team: Poems about Baseball* (Grayson Books.) He has received poetry fellowships from the National Endowment for the Arts, the National Endowment for the Humanities, the New Jersey State Arts Council, and the Pennsylvania State Arts Council. He received the 2013 New Jersey Poetry Prize for his poem, "Champion" and Garrison Keillor has twice featured Romond's poetry on NPR's *The Writer's Almanac*.

John Rossi is Professor Emeritus of History at La Salle University in Philadelphia. He has written extensively about the career of George Orwell, most recently "The Catholic Who Knew Orwell," Modern Age, Spring, 2019.

Javanse' Ryland-Buntley lives in Rochester, NY. Her most recent fiction appeared in *Jigsaw*.

Matilda Schieren is a writer and B2B marketer based in Oak Park, Illinois. She's a proud Villanova alumna and devout Philadelphia sports fan who takes cheesesteak evangelism quite seriously.

Fereshteh Sholevar, an Iranian born poet and writer, immigrated to Germany and later to the USA in 1978. She earned her Master's degree in Creative writing at the University of Iowa and Rosemont College, PA. She writes in four languages, has authored six books, which include a novel and a children's book, and has won awards from Philadelphia poets and PA Poetry Society. Her new bilingual poetry collection, *Of Dust And Chocolate*, (English-French) is available at Amazon.

Until recently, **John Timpane** was the Commentary Page Editor and later the Theater Critic and Books Editor of The Philadelphia Inquirer. His work has appeared in *Sequoia, Cleaver, The Painted Bride Quarterly, Vocabula Review, Per Contra, Apiary*, and elsewhere.

Josie Tolin is an Indiana native and recent graduate of the University of Michigan. Her short fiction has also appeared in *Jersey Devil Press*. Thankfully, she does not have a peanut allergy.

Pete Tonery no longer works in marketing but makes images and writes drama, essays and fiction. He lives on a small sustainable farm in rural Monroe County, NY. He and his spouse raise vegetables, chickens and occasionally pork. Four time winner of the GEVA Theater Regional Playwrights Festival; recently, photography published in *Grey Sparrow Review*.

Joseph Howard Tyson graduated from LaSalle University with a B.A. in Philosophy, took graduate courses in English at Pennsylvania State University, then served in the U. S. Marine Corps. He lives in a Philadelphia suburb, and works in the insurance industry. In addition to non-fiction articles published in *Schuylkill Valley Journal, Southern Cross Review*, and other publications, he has written six books: *Penn's Luminous City* (2005), *Madame Blavatsky Revisited* (2006), *Hitler's Mentor: Dietrich Eckart* (2008), *The Surreal Reich* (2010), *World War II Leaders* (2011), and *Fifty-Seven Years of Russian Madness* (2015). Tyson is currently working on a satiric dictionary.

Cleveland Wall is a poet, editor, and teaching artist from Bethlehem, PA. She is one half of the poetry-guitar duo The Starry Eyes and a founding member of the poetry improv group No River Twice. Cleveland also cohosts Tuesday Muse, a monthly poetry and music series at Bethlehem's Ice House.

Kelsey Wang is a junior at Taipei American School. She is the head editor of her school's literary magazine, *Expression*, and her work has been recognized by Scholastic Art & Writing Awards. When she is not writing, she can be found playing the piano, agonizing over math problems, or drawing very badly. In general, she spends too much time daydreaming. She lives in Taipei, Taiwan, with her extended family.

Shamon Williams is an African American student at the University of Central Florida pursuing a BS in psychology and a BA in English. When she isn't working, writing or taking yet another nap, she partakes in acting, modeling, aerial dance or video games. She strives to become a bestselling novelist and/or an Oscar-winning actress. Shamon's work has been published in *Cypress Dome* and *Dreamers Creative Writing*.

"Catfish" John Wojtowicz grew up working on his family's azalea and rhododendron nursery in the backwoods of what Ginsberg dubbed "nowhere Zen New Jersey." He has been featured in the Philadelphia based *Moonstone Poetry* series, West Chester based *Livin' on Luck* series, and Rowan University's Writer's Roundtable on 89.7 WGLS-FM. Recent publications: *Jelly Bucket, Tule Review, The Patterson Literary Review, Montana Mouthful, Driftwood,* and *Glassworks*.

Schuylkill Valley Journal

—Submission Guidelines—

Schuylkill Valley Journal is published as both a print and online journal. *SVJ* print is released twice a year, in spring and fall. *SVJ* online (svjlit.com) is published on a more frequent basis. *SVJ* publishes short stories, flash fiction, interviews, photography, cityscapes, critical essays and features on art and sculpture (especially Philadelphia sculpture). *SVJ* also publishes poetry; however, all poetry will first appear in *SVJ* print.

All submissions (except poetry) should be sent through the website to svj.query@gmail.com. Please see separate information for poetry below. We prefer previously unpublished work though published work is acceptable (indicate where previously published). Simultaneous submissions are OK (please notify us if your work is published elsewhere). All submissions will be considered for both our print and online journals. Our aim in reviewing material that is first considered for *SVJ* online (material other than poetry and longer short stories) is to inform writers of the status of their inquiry within two weeks.

Submissions should be sent in .doc or .rtf file format only in Times New Roman, 12-point font, and single-spaced and should include title, author name, bio and complete text, including any notes regarding previous publication. In the subject line all submissions should state the submission type (e.g., short story, flash fiction, essay) and include the writer's full name, and contact information. Any file not meeting these specifications may not be read. Manuscripts will not be returned. All submissions except poetry should include a word count.

Poetry: Because of the high volume of poetry we receive, we have both a separate submission address and different guidelines from our other genres. Please visit our website to read all Poetry guidelines before submitting, and send poems directly to the poetry editor, Bernadette McBride, at PoetrySVJ@gmail.com.

Short Stories and Flash Fiction: 1-2 stories (if more than 3,000 words please only submit one). Flash fiction (preferably 500-1,000 words); short stories no more than 6,000 words. Submissions will be considered for both the online and print journal, with the exception of short stories greater than 2,000 words (*SVJ* print only). We like fiction that explores a situation or illuminates a character. We look for original use of language, fresh voices, and diversity. We also seek writers who have insights into the mysteries of everyday life, relationships and the world around us. Stories can pose questions and answer them or not; however, they must be well-crafted. Stories can be sent through the website to query.svj@gmail.com or can be sent via snail mail. The preferred method is via snail mail. Stories sent by snail mail should be typed, double-spaced, one side only with name, address, word count and bio on first page. Send to:

Fran Metzman
Fiction Editor, *Schuylkill Valley Journal*
1900 JFK Blvd, /2012
Philadelphia, PA 19103

Essays and Interviews: 5,000 words max. (preferably under 2,000 words for *SVJ* on-line) on topics of literary or artistic interest, personal reflections, interviews, etc.). Submissions should incude the word count and bio on first page. Inquiry to email address (macpoet1@aol.com) is always advisable. Queries should include a concept/abstract of the proposed article, approximately a paragraph. All submissions will be sent through query.svj@gmail.com. All articles and non-fiction pieces will be assigned by editor.

—Copyright—

Material that appears in *Schuylkill Valley Journal* (print and online) is the copyright of the contributor. By submitting a work to *SVJ*, the contributor agrees that *Schuylkill Valley Journal* reserves first rights, and the right to retain the material in our archives indefinitely. It may also be used in reference to previous issues and be included in future *SVJ* endeavors. All other rights belong to the contributor. *SVJ* online does not claim ownership of syndicated material from other sources, and proper credit will be given as necessary. We request the same courtesy from our peers. All rights are similarly reserved by *Schuylkill Valley Journal*.

—Payment—

For contributors to *SVJ* print, payment is one copy of the journal in which your work appears. Additional copies are $10 each. All rights revert to authors upon publication. The cost of *Schuylkill Valley Journal* is $10 an issue and $13 if sent via mail. For other information about *SVJ*, contact Peter Krok, the publisher and Editor-in-Chief of *SVJ*, and Humanities Director of the Manayunk-Roxborough Art Center (MRAC), at macpoet1@aol.com or by phone at 215-482-3363 (MRAC) or 610-609-1490 (cell).

—Subscription Form—
Schuylkill Valley Journal

Name: _____

Street Address:_____

City, State, Zip Code: _____

Phone: _____

Subscriptions: ( ) One Year $23*   ( ) Two Years $45*

(includes postage)   (includes postage)

For an issue that contains my work:

( )   Send my payment copies with my subscription copy.

( )   Send my payment copies and transfer my subscription to the next issue.

Contributions

( ) $10   ( ) $25   ( ) $50   ( ) $100   ( ) Other

Please make checks payable to
Peter Krok – *Schuylkill Valley Journal*

and mail to:
Peter Krok, 240 Golf Hills Road, Havertown, PA 19083

*For subscriptions that do not require postage, a one year subscription is $20 and a two year subscription is $40.

Made in the USA
Lexington, KY
03 December 2019